WAY TO HAPPINESS

ST PAULS / SHEEN BOOKS

Calvary and the Mass
Children and Parents
The Divine Romance
The Eternal Galilean
Guide to Contentment
Old Errors and New Labels
The Prodigal World
The Rock Plunged Into Eternity
The Seven Capital Sins
The Seven Last Words
Those Mysterious Priests
Thoughts for Daily Living
Walk With God
The Way of the Cross
Way to Happiness
Way to Inner Peace
You

BOOKS ABOUT ARCHBISHOP FULTON J. SHEEN

Fulton J. Sheen by Kathleen L. Riley
The Spiritual Legacy of Archbishop Fulton J. Sheen
by Rev. Charles P. Connor

Way to Happiness

*An Inspiring Guide to
Peace, Hope and Contentment*

FULTON J. SHEEN, PhD, DD

*Agrégé en Philosophie de L'Université de Louvain and
The Catholic University of America*

ST PAULS

Library of Congress Cataloging-in-Publication Data

Sheen, Fulton J. (Fulton John), 1895-1979.
    Way to Happiness: an inspiring guide to peace, hope, and
contentment / Fulton J. Sheen.
        p.   cm.
    Originally published: New York: Maco Magazine Corp., 1953.
    ISBN 0-8189-0775-4
    1. Christian life — Catholic authors.   I. Title.
BX2350.S53   1998
    248.4'82 — dc21   97-19481
                                                                CIP

ISBN 10: 0-8189-0775-4
ISBN 13: 978-0-8189-0775-5

This Alba House edition is produced by special arrangement
with the Estate of Fulton J. Sheen and the Society for the
Propagation of the Faith, 366 Fifth Avenue, New York, NY 10001. It
has been revised to incorporate a more recent and more recognizable
translation of the Scripture texts.

This book is published in the United States of America
by Alba House, the publishing arm of the Society of St. Paul,
an international religious congregation of priests and brothers
serving the Church through the communications media.

Current Printing - first digit   8   9   10   11   12

Place of Publication:
2187 Victory Blvd., Staten Island, NY 10314 - USA

Year of Current Printing - first year shown

                              2014   2015   2016   2017   2018   2019

TABLE OF CONTENTS

Youth

Inner Peace

Giving

Man

Introduction

PLAN AND PURPOSE

THIS MATERIAL HAS BEEN WRITTEN with a particular purpose in mind, a special method, and a deliberate spirit. The purpose will be to bring solace, healing and hope to hearts; truth and enlightenment to minds; goodness, strength and resolution to wills. The method will be the application of eternal moral and spiritual principles to the basic problems of individual and social life today. The spirit will be that of charity: love of God and love of neighbor.

And this preface will declare the basic assumptions of this book.

First: The overemphasis on politics today is an indication that people are governed, rather than governing. The complexities of our civilization force us to organize into larger and larger units; we have become so intent on governing what is outside of us that we neglect to govern our own selves. Yet the key to social betterment is always to be found in personal betterment. Remake man and you remake his world. We gravely need to restore to man his self-respect and to give him his appropriate honor: this will keep him from bowing cravenly before those who threaten to enslave him, and it will give him the courage to defend the right, alone if need be, when the world is wrong.

Second: As society is made by man, so man, in his turn, is made by his thoughts, his decisions and his choices. Nothing ever happens to the world which did not first happen inside the mind of some man: the material of the skyscraper merely completes the architect's dream. Even the material of our physical selves is the servant of our thoughts: psychologists recognize the fact that our bodies may become tired only because of tiredness in the mind. Worry, anxiety, fear and boredom are felt as physical: mind-fatigue oftentimes results in bodily fatigue.

One basic reason for tiredness of mind is the conflict in all of us between ideal and achievement, between what we ought to be and what we are, between our longing and our having, between our powers of understanding and the incomprehensible mysteries of the universe. A house divided against itself cannot stand; this perennial tension in man can be accepted and made bearable only by a surrender of the self to God. Then whatever happens is welcomed as a gift of love: frustration cannot happen to us for we have no clamorous, selfish will.

Society can be saved only if man is saved from his unbearable conflicts, and man can be rescued from them only if his soul is saved. Once, not so long ago, men put their hope of happiness in material advance. Now that mood of shallow optimism has ended; the heavy burden of worry and anxiety about the future of the race and of the individual has made men conscious of their souls.

Third: Our happiness consists in fulfilling the purpose of our being. Every man knows, from his own unfulfilled hunger for them, that he was built with a capacity for three things of which he never has enough. He wants *life* — not for the next few minutes, but for always, and with no aging or disease to threaten it. He also wants to grasp *truth* — not with a forced choice between the truths of mathematics or geography, but he wants all truth. Thirdly, he wants *love* — not with a time-limit, not mixed with satiety or disillusionment, but love that will be an abiding ecstasy.

These three things are not to be found in this life in their completion: on earth life is shadowed by death, truth mingles with error, love is mixed with hate. But men know they would not long for these things in their purity if there were no possibility of ever finding them. So, being reasonable, they search for the source from which these mixed and imperfect portions of life, love, and truth derive.

The search is like looking for the source of light in a room: it cannot come from under a chair, where light is mixed with darkness and shadow. But it can come from the sun, where light is pure with neither shadow nor darkness dulling it. In looking for the source of love, light, truth, as we know it here, we must go out beyond the limits of this shadowed world — to a Truth not mingled with its shadow, error — to a Life not mingled with its shadow, death — to a Love not mingled with its shadow, hate. We must seek for Pure Life, Pure Truth and Pure Love — and that is the definition of God. His Life is personal enough to be a Father; His Truth is personal and comprehensible enough to be a Son; His Love is so deep and spiritual that it is a Spirit.

When enough men have found this way to happiness, they will find one another in brotherhood. Social peace will then ensue.

Fulton J. Sheen

Biblical Abbreviations

OLD TESTAMENT

Genesis	Gn	Nehemiah	Ne	Baruch	Ba
Exodus	Ex	Tobit	Tb	Ezekiel	Ezk
Leviticus	Lv	Judith	Jdt	Daniel	Dn
Numbers	Nb	Esther	Est	Hosea	Ho
Deuteronomy	Dt	1 Maccabees	1 M	Joel	Jl
Joshua	Jos	2 Maccabees	2 M	Amos	Am
Judges	Jg	Job	Jb	Obadiah	Ob
Ruth	Rt	Psalms	Ps	Jonah	Jon
1 Samuel	1 S	Proverbs	Pr	Micah	Mi
2 Samuel	2 S	Ecclesiastes	Ec	Nahum	Na
1 Kings	1 K	Song of Songs	Sg	Habakkuk	Hab
2 Kings	2 K	Wisdom	Ws	Zephaniah	Zp
1 Chronicles	1 Ch	Sirach	Si	Haggai	Hg
2 Chronicles	2 Ch	Isaiah	Is	Malachi	Ml
Ezra	Ezr	Jeremiah	Jr	Zechariah	Zc
		Lamentations	Lm		

NEW TESTAMENT

Matthew	Mt	Ephesians	Eph	Hebrews	Heb
Mark	Mk	Philippians	Ph	James	Jm
Luke	Lk	Colossians	Col	1 Peter	1 P
John	Jn	1 Thessalonians	1 Th	2 Peter	2 P
Acts	Ac	2 Thessalonians	2 Th	1 John	1 Jn
Romans	Rm	1 Timothy	1 Tm	2 John	2 Jn
1 Corinthians	1 Cor	2 Timothy	2 Tm	3 John	3 Jn
2 Corinthians	2 Cor	Titus	Tt	Jude	Jude
Galatians	Gal	Philemon	Phm	Revelation	Rv

WAY TO HAPPINESS

1

CONTENTMENT

CONTENTMENT IS NOT AN innate virtue. It is acquired through great resolution and diligence in conquering unruly desires; hence it is an art which few study. Because there are millions of discontented souls in the world today, it might be helpful for them to analyze the four main causes of discontent, and to suggest means to contentment.

The principal cause of discontent is *egotism*, or selfishness, which sets the self up as a primary plant around which everyone else must revolve. The second cause of discontent is *envy*, which makes us regard the possessions and the talents of others as if they were stolen from us. The third cause is *covetousness*, or an inordinate desire to have more, in order to compensate for the emptiness of our heart. The fourth cause of discontent is *jealousy*, which is sometimes occasioned through melancholia and sadness, and at other times by a hatred of those who have what we wish for ourselves.

One of the greatest mistakes is to think that contentment comes from something outside us rather than from a quality of the soul. There was once a boy who only wanted a marble; when he had a marble, he only wanted a ball; when he had a ball, he only wanted a top; when he had a top, he only wanted a kite, and when he had the marble, the ball, the top, and the kite, he still was not happy. Trying to make a discontented person happy is like trying to fill a sieve with water. However much you pour into it, it runs out too rapidly for you to catch up.

Nor is contentment to be found in an exchange of places. There are some who believe that if they were in a different part of the earth they would have a greater peace of soul. A goldfish, in a globe of water, and a canary in a cage, on a hot day, began talking. The fish said: "I wish I could swing like that canary; I'd like to be up there in that cage." And the canary said: "Oh, how nice to be down in that cool water where the fish is." Suddenly a voice said: "Canary, go down to the water! Fish, go up to the cage!" Immediately, they exchanged places, but neither was happy, because God originally had given each a place according to his ability, one that best suited his own nature.

The condition of our contentment is to be contained, to recognize limits. Whatever is within limits is likely to be quiet. A walled garden is one of the quietest places in the world; the world is shut out, and through its gates one can look upon it with the affection of distance, borrowing enchantment from it. So, if the soul of man is kept within limits (that is to say, not avaricious, greedy, over-reaching or selfish), it, too, is shut into a calm, quiet, sunny contentment. Contented man, limited and bound by circumstances, makes those very limits the cure of his restlessness. It is not to the point whether a garden has one acre or three, or whether or not it has a wall; what matters is that we shall live within its bounds, whether they be large or small, in order that we can possess a quiet spirit and a happy heart.

Contentment, therefore, comes in part from *faith* — that is, from knowing the purpose of life and being assured that whatever the trials are, they come from the hand of a loving Father. Secondly, in order to have contentment one must also have *a good conscience*. If the inner self is unhappy because of moral failures and unatoned guilt, then nothing external can give rest to the spirit. A third and final need is *mortification of desires*, the limitation of delights. What we over-love, we often over-grieve. Contentment enhances our enjoyment and diminishes our misery. All evils become lighter if we endure them patiently, but the greatest benefits can be poisoned by discontent. The miseries of life are sufficiently deep and extensive, without our adding to them unnecessarily.

Contentment with our worldly condition is not inconsistent with the desire for betterment. To the poorest man, Christianity says not to be merely content, but "be diligent in business." The contentment enjoined is for the time being. Man is poor today, and for this day, faith enjoins him to be satisfied; but deliverance from his poverty may be best for tomorrow, and therefore the poor man works for his increased prosperity. He may not succeed; if his poverty continues for another day, he accepts it, and then proceeds until relief comes. Thus, contentment is relative to our present state, and is not absolute in respect to the entire demands of our nature. A contented man is never poor though he have very, very little. The discontented man is never rich, let him have so very much.

2

REDUCING EGO TO ZERO

THE CHIEF CAUSE OF INNER unhappiness is egotism or selfishness. He who gives himself importance by boasting is actually showing the credentials of his own worthlessness. Pride is an attempt to create an impression that we are what we actually are not.

How much happier people would be if instead of exalting their ego to infinity, they reduced it to zero. They would then find the true infinite through the rarest of modern virtues: humility. Humility is truth about ourselves. A man who is six feet tall, but who says: "I am only five feet tall," is not humble. He who is a good writer is not humble if he says: "I am a scribbler." Such statements are made in order that there might be a denial and thus win praise. Rather he would be humbler who says: "Well, whatever talent I have is a gift of God and I thank Him for it." The higher the building the deeper the foundation; the greater the moral heights to which we aspire the greater the humility. As John the Baptist said when he saw Our Lord: "I must decrease; He must increase." Flowers humbly depart in the winter to see their mother roots. Dead to the world, they keep house under the earth in humble humility, unseen by the eyes of men. But because they humbled themselves, they are exalted and glorified in the new springtime.

Only when a box is empty can it be filled; only when the ego is deflated can God pour in His blessings. Some are already so stuffed with their own ego that it is impossible for love of neighbor or love of God to enter. By seeking their own constantly, everyone disowns them. But humility makes us receptive to the giving of others. You could not give unless I took. It is the taker that makes the giver. So God, before He can be Giver, must find a taker. But if one is not humble enough to receive from God, then he receives nothing.

A man possessed by the Devil was brought to a Father of the Desert. When the saint commanded the Devil to leave, the Devil asked: "What is the difference between the sheep and the goats whom the Lord will put at His right and His left Hand on the day of Judgment?" The saint answered: "I am one of the goats." The Devil said: "I leave because of your humility."

Many say: "I have labored for years for others and even for God, and what did I get out of it? I am still nothing." The answer is, they have gained something; they have gained the truth of their own littleness — and of course, great merit in the next life. One day two men were in a carriage. One said: "There is not enough room for you here in this seat." The other said: "We will love each other a little more, and then there will be room enough." Ask a man: "Are you a saint?" If he answers in the affirmative, you can be very sure that he is not.

The humble man concentrates on his own errors, and not upon those of others; he sees nothing in his neighbor but what is good and virtuous. He does not carry his own faults on his back, but in front of him. The neighbor's defects he carries in a sack on his back, so he will not see them. The proud man, on the contrary, complains against everybody and believes that he has been wronged or else not treated as he deserves. When the humble man is treated badly he does not complain for he knows that he is treated better than he deserves. From a spiritual point of view, he who is proud of his intelligence, talent or voice, and never thanks God for them is a robber; he has taken gifts from God and never recognized the Giver. The ears of barley which bear the richest grain always hang the lowest. The humble man is never discouraged, but the proud man falls into despair. The humble man still has God to call upon; the proud man has only his own ego that has collapsed.

One of the loveliest prayers for humility is that of Saint Francis: "Lord, make me an instrument of Your peace. Where there is hatred, let there be love;

where there is injury, pardon; where there is doubt, faith; where there is despair, hope; where there is darkness, light; where there is sadness, joy. O Divine Master, grant that I may seek, not so much to be consoled as to console; to be understood as to understand; to be loved as to love. For it is in giving that we receive, it is in pardoning that we are pardoned, and it is in dying that we are born to Eternal Life."

3

JOY

JOY IS THE DELIGHTFUL EXPERIENCE of the feelings of pleasure at a good gained and actually enjoyed or the prospect of good which one has a reasonable hope of obtaining. There can be both natural joys and spiritual joys. Natural joys would be the joy of youth before disappointment has stretched the soul, or the joy of health when food is pleasant and sweet, or the joy of success when the battle has been won, or the joys of affection when the heart is loved. All these natural joys are intensified by spiritual joys and put upon a more enduring basis. No earthly happiness would be permanent or thorough if it were not associated with a good conscience.

Spiritual joy is a serenity of temper in the midst of the changes of life, such as a mountain has when a storm breaks over it. To a man who has never rooted the soul in the Divine every trouble exaggerates itself. He cannot put his full powers to any one thing because he is troubled about many things.

A joy is not the same as levity. Levity is an act; joy, a habit. Mirth is like a meteor, cheerfulness like a star; mirth is like crackling thorns, joy like a fire. Joy being more permanent makes difficult actions easier. Soldiers after a long day's march would hardly walk as nimbly as they do, if they did not march to music. A cheerful heart always finds a yoke easy and a burden light.

Certainly no nurse is helpful in a sick room unless she has the spirit of cheerfulness. Every nurse really ought to have two things before she enters a sick room: an incision and a sense of humor. An incision in order that she may know the value of pain; a sense of humor in order that she may know how to diffuse happiness. This incision need not be physical but it should at least be symbolic, in the sense that there should be a deep appreciation of the woes and sufferings of others. There is nothing that so much adds to the longevity of sickness as a long face.

Joy has much more to do with the affections than with reason. To the man with a family his wife and children call out and sustain his delights much more than his intellect could ever stimulate. Standing before a cradle a father seems face to face with the attributes of the everlasting Being Who has infused His tenderness and love into the babe. The power of rejoicing is always a fair test of a man's moral condition. No man can be happy on the outside who is already unhappy on the inside. If a sense of guilt weighs down the soul no amount of pleasure on the outside can compensate for the loss of joy on the inside. As sorrow is attendant on sin, so joy is the companion of holiness.

Joy can be felt in both prosperity and adversity. In prosperity it consists not in the goods we enjoy but in those we hope for; not in the pleasures we experience but in the promise of those which we believe without our seeing. Riches may abound but those for which we hope are the kind which moths do not eat, rust consume, nor thieves break through and steal. Even in adversity there can be joy in the assurance that the Divine Master Himself died through the Cross as the condition of His Resurrection.

If joy be uncommon today it is because there are timid souls who have not the courage to forget themselves and to make sacrifices for their neighbor, or else because the narrower sympathies make the brighter things of the world to come, appear as vanities. As the pull from the belief in God and the salvation of the soul fade from life, so also joy vanishes and one returns to the despair of the heathens. The old Greeks and Romans always saw a shadow across their path and a skeleton at their feet. It was no surprise that one day a Roman who had nothing to live for, nothing to hope for, entered his bath and opened a vein and so bled quietly and painlessly to death. A famous Greek poet once said of life that it was better not to be born, and the next best thing was to quit life as soon as possible. All this is at the other extreme from St. Paul, who said: "Rejoice in the Lord always; again I say, Rejoice!" (Ph 4:4).

4

Is Modern Man Far From Peace?

No one is dangerously unhappy except the individual who does not know what happiness means. Life is unbearable only to those who are ignorant of why they are alive. Men in such a condition of soul equate happiness with pleasure (which is a very different matter) and identify joy with a tingling of the nerve-endings (which it is not). But things which are external to us never bring us inner peace. The more persistently anyone looks for satisfaction and a goal to serve in something outside of his control, the less stable he will find it, the more subject he will be to disappointments.

There are two movements towards happiness. The first of these is our withdrawal from the outside — from too great an absorption in the things of the world. The second movement is far more profound: it is an ascension from what is inferior within us to what is its superior, from our egotism to our God. Modern man has experienced the first movement; exterior things have become so many sources of misery to him. Wars, depressions, the insecurity and emptiness of life have so terrified men that they have tried to close off their contacts with the outside world and have begun to seek for satisfactions in their own limited selves. That is why psychiatry is having such a field-day: the modern soul, alarmed at what it finds without, has drawn down the shades and begun to look for contentment in analyzing its own unconsciousness, anxieties and fears, its doldrums and frustrations.

But such self-containment can prove a prison if one is locked into it with his own ego alone, for there is no more confining strait-jacket in the world than that of the self left to itself. The cure never lies in using a psychoanalytic scalpel to release the inner moral pus and watch it flow; that is a morbid act for both the patient and the doctor. The cure, rather, consists in discovering why one is lonely, and afraid of solitude — for most people have a dread of being alone, without knowing why the prospect frightens them.

The problem of our day is this problem of finding interior peace, and it is in this that the twentieth century is marked off from the nineteenth. A hundred years ago men looked to the exterior world for the answers to their problems: they worshipped science or nature, expected happiness to come from progress or politics or profits. The twentieth century man is worried about himself: he is even more concerned over the problem of sex than by sex itself — is interested in the mental attitude he should take towards it, rather than in its physical satisfaction and the begetting of children. His own values, moods and attitudes absorb him.

Although a great deal of nonsense has been written about the interior life of men in our day, it is still true that the twentieth century is closer to God than the nineteenth century was. We are living on the eve of one of the great spiritual revivals of human history. Souls are sometimes closest to God when they feel themselves farthest away from Him, at the point of despair. For an empty soul, the Divine can fill; a worried soul, the Infinite can pacify. A self-concerned, proud soul, however, is inaccessible to grace.

Modern man has been humiliated: neither his proud expectations of progress nor of science have turned out as he hoped. Yet he has not quite reached the point of humbling himself. He is still imprisoned in the self, and able to see nothing else beyond. The psychoanalysts may be allowed to bore into his thoughts for a few years more; but the time is not far off when modern men will utter a frantic appeal to God to lift them from the empty cistern of their own egos. St. Augustine knew it well: he said, "Our hearts are restless until they rest in You."

That is why — although a catastrophic war may threaten us — the times are not as bad as they seem. Modern man has not yet returned to God; but he has, at least, returned to himself. Later he will surpass and transcend himself with God's grace, which he is seeking, even now. No one ever looked for something unless he knew that it existed; today the frustrated soul is looking for God, as for the memory of a name he used to know.

The difference between those who have found God in faith and those who are still seeking Him is like the difference between a wife, happy in the enjoyment of her husband's companionship, and a young girl wondering if she will ever find a husband, and perhaps trying to attract men by the wrong approach. Those who search for pleasure, fame and wealth are all seeking the Infinite, but the seekers are still on the outskirts of the Eternal City. Those with faith have penetrated to their real home within the Infinite and have found the "peace which the world cannot give." As one can see a figure far off and not yet recognize him as a long-lost friend, so one can sense the need of the Infinite and desire the endless ecstasy of love, but not yet know that it is God.

It makes no difference how wicked a soul may be, there is no one subjecting himself to illicit pleasures who does not have a consciousness of his subjection and his slavery. Perhaps that is why alcoholics are often liars; their lips deny a slavery which their lives so visibly witness. Such individuals, unwilling to admit themselves mistaken, still refuse to be convinced of Divine Truth; but their sadness and their emptiness will eventually drive them to the God of Mercy.

Our exterior world today is in desperate straits, but the inner world of man is far from hopeless. The world of politics and economics lags behind the psychological development of men themselves. The world is far from God, but human hearts are not. That is why peace will come less from political changes than from man himself, who, driven to take refuge within his own soul from the turmoil without, will be lifted above himself to the happiness for which he was made.

5

JOY FROM THE INSIDE

EACH OF US MAKES HIS OWN weather, determines the color of the skies in the emotional universe which he inhabits. We can, by a creative effort, bring such sunlight to our souls that it makes radiant whatever events may come our way. We can, on the other hand, permit ourselves to slump into a state of inner depression so deep and filled with gloom that only the most intense outward stimulations of the senses are able to rouse us from our apathy.

Everyone must have pleasure, the philosophers tell us. The man who has integrated his personality in accordance with its nature, and oriented his life towards God knows the intense and indestructible pleasure the saints called joy. No outward event can threaten him or ruffle his happiness. But many men look outward for their pleasure and expect the accidents of their lives to provide their happiness. Since nobody can make the universe his slave, everyone who looks outward for pleasure is bound to disappointment. A glut of entertainment wearies us; a realized ambition becomes a bore; a love that promised full contentment loses its glamor and its thrill. Lasting happiness can never come from the world. Joy is not derived from the things we get or the people we meet; it is manufactured by the soul itself, as it goes about its self-forgetful business.

The secret of a happy life is the moderation of our pleasures in exchange for an increase of joy. But several contemporary practices make this difficult for us. One of these is the type of merchandising which tries to increase our desires in order that we shall buy more goods. Allied with this is the "spoiled-child" psychology of modern man, which tells him that he is entitled to get anything he wants, that the world owes everyone the satisfaction of his whims. Once the ego has become the center around which everything else revolves, we are vulnerable: our peace can be destroyed by a draft from an open window, by our inability to buy a coat made of some exotic fur so rare that only twenty women in the world can wear it — by our failure to get invited to a luncheon, or our failure to pay the biggest income tax in the nation. The ego is always insatiable, if it is in command; no indulgences and no honors quiet its craving, either for "madder music and for a stronger wine," or for the heady delights of testimonial dinners and 72-point headlines.

The ego-centered men view as calamities the denial of any of their wishes: they want to dominate their world, to pull its puppet-strings and force those about them to obey their will. If such an ego's wishes are crossed and checked by another ego, its owner is in despair. Occasions for despondency and sadness are thus multiplied, for all of us are bound to be denied some of the things we want — it is our choice whether this loss shall be accepted with a cheerful good grace or taken as an outrage and an affront to us.

Today millions of men and women consider that their happiness is destroyed if they must get along without a few things of which their grandfathers had never dreamed. Luxuries have become necessities to them; and the more things a man needs in order to be happy, the more he has increased his chances of disappointment and despair. Whim has become his master, trivia his tyrant; he no longer is self-possessed, but he has become possessed by outward objects, trumpery toys.

Plato in his *Republic* wrote of the man whose life is run by his whims and fancies; his words were written 2,400 years ago, but they are still pertinent today: "Often he will take to politics, leaping to his feet, and do or say whatever comes into his head; or he conceives an admiration for a general and his interests turn to war; or for a man of business, and straightway that is his line. He knows no order or necessity in life; he will not listen to anyone who tells him that some pleasures come in the gratification of good and noble desires, others from evil ones, and that the former should be fostered and encouraged, the latter disciplined and chained. To all such talk, he shakes his head and says that all enthusiasms are similar and worthy of equal attention."

Pleasures must be arranged in a hierarchy if we are to get the greatest enjoyment out of life. The most intense and lasting joys come only to those who are willing to practice a certain self-restraint, to undergo the boredom of a preliminary discipline. The best view is from the mountain-top, but it may be arduous to reach it. No man ever enjoyed reading Horace without drilling himself with the declensions of his grammar first. Full happiness is understood only by those who have denied themselves some legitimate pleasures in order to obtain deferred joys. Men who "let themselves go," go to seed or go mad. The Savior of the world Himself told us that the best joys come only after we have purchased them by prayer and fasting: we must give up our copper pennies first, out of love for Him, and He will pay us back in pieces of gold, in joy and ecstasy.

6

LOVE IS INFINITE

THERE IS A PROFOUND DIFFERENCE in quality between the possessions that we need, and use, and actually enjoy, and the accumulation of useless things we accumulate out of vanity or greed or the desire to surpass others. The first kind of possession is a legitimate extension of our personalities: we enrich a much-used object by our love, and it becomes dear to us. We can learn about the two kinds of ownership in any nursery: a child who has only a single toy enriches it with his love. The spoiled child, with many play-things spread out for him, quickly becomes blasé and ceases to take pleasure in any one of them. The quality of his love diminishes with the number of objects offered for his love… as a river has less depth, the more it spreads over the plains.

When we visit a large mansion, inhabited by only two people, we feel the coldness of such a house, too vast to be made a home by human love. Each of us, by his presence, can ennoble a few cubic feet… but no more. The more people own beyond the limit of things they can personalize and love, the more they will suffer boredom, ennui and satiety.

Yet men and women are forever trying to add to their possessions far beyond the limit of enjoyment. This is because of their mistaken belief that their hunger for Infinity can be satisfied by an infinity of material things: what they really wish for is the Infinity of Divine Love.

Our imaginations are easily misled into desiring a false infinity, when once we begin to long for "wealth." For "wealth" and "money" are things that appeal to the imagination, which is insatiable in its wishes. Real goods, such as those our bodies need, have not this quality: there is a narrow limit to the amount of food our stomachs will hold and when that is reached, we do not wish for more. Our Lord fed the five thousand in the desert with fish and bread, and all of them had their fill. But if He had given them, instead, a $20,000 bond, no single person would have said, "One is enough for me."

Credit-wealth — stocks, bonds, bank-balances — have no set limit, at which we say, "No more." They have in them a caricature infinity, which allows men to use them as false religions, as substitutes for the true Infinity of God. Like money, love and power can become ersatz religions: those who pursue these things as ends will never find satisfaction. Such men are all in pursuit of God, but they do not know His name, nor where to look for Him.

Since every increase in quantity among the things we love brings a decrease in the quality of love, there are two ways by which we may hope to keep love pure. One is to give away in proportion as we receive: this habit reminds us that we are merely trustees of God's riches, not their rightful owners. Yet few people risk doing this: they are afraid to touch their "capital," and every cent they add to it becomes part of the sacred pile which must not be disturbed. They become identified with what they love; if it is wealth, they cannot bear to part with any portion of its accumulated burden.

The second way of preserving ourselves from an unseemly greed is the heroic way... the way of complete detachment from wealth, as practiced by St. Francis of Assisi and all those who take the vows of poverty. There is a paradox in such a renunciation, for the man who has given up even the hope of "security" is the richest man in the world; he is the most secure of all of us, for he wants nothing... and that is a boast that no millionaire can make. Everyone's power of renunciation is greater than anyone's power to possess: no man can own the earth, but any man can disown it.

Misers may fill their wallets, but never their hearts, for they cannot obtain all the wealth they are able to imagine and desire. But the poor in heart are rich in happiness. God gave us love enough to spend in getting back to Him so that we could find Infinity there; He did not give us love enough to hoard.

7

THE PHILOSOPHY OF PLEASURE

WE ALL WANT HAPPINESS. We should all take the sensible step of learning that there are three laws of pleasure which, if followed, will make the attainment of happiness immeasurably easier.

The first law: *If you are ever to have a good time, you cannot plan your life to include nothing but good times*. Pleasure is like beauty; it is conditioned by contrast. A woman who wants to show off her black velvet dress will not, if she is wise, stand against a black curtain, but against a white backdrop. She wants the contrast. Fireworks would not delight us if they were shot off against a background of fire, or in the blaze of the noonday sun: they need to stand out against the darkness. Lilies bring us a special pleasure because their petals rise, surprisingly, on the waters of foul ponds. Contrast is needed to help us see each thing as being vividly itself.

Pleasure, by the same principle, is best enjoyed when it comes to us as a "treat," in contrast to experiences that are less pleasurable. We make a great mistake if we try to have all our nights party-nights. No one would enjoy Thanksgiving if every meal were a turkey dinner. New Year's Eve would not delight us if the whistles blew at midnight every night.

Fun rests on contrast, and so does the enjoyment of a funny situation. If a Bishop has a miter thrust on the side of his head by an errant master of ceremonies, it makes us laugh; it would not be funny if all Bishops always wore their miters askew.

Our enjoyment of life is vastly increased if we follow the spiritual injunction to bring some mortification and self-denial into our lives. This practice saves us from being jaded; it preserves the tang and joy of living. The harp-strings of our lives are not thin, made slack by being pulled until they are out of tune; instead, we tighten them and help preserve their harmony.

Self-discipline brings back to us the excitement of our childhood, when our pleasures were rationed — when we got our dessert at the end of the meal and never at the start.

The second law: *Pleasure is deepened and enhanced when it has survived a moment of tedium or pain.* This law helps us to make our prized pleasures last for a whole lifetime. To do so, we must keep going at anything we do until we get our second wind. One enjoys a mountain-climb more after passing through the first moment of discouraged exhaustion. One becomes more interested in a job or work after the first impulse to drop it has been overcome.

In the same way, marriages become stable only after disillusionment has brought the honeymoon to an end. The great value of the marital vow is in keeping the couple together during the first quarrel; it tides them over their early period of resentment, until they get the second wind of true happiness at being together. Married joys, like all great joys, are born out of some pain. As we must crack the nut to taste the sweet so, in the spiritual life, the cross must be the prelude to the crown.

The third law: *Pleasure is a by-product, not a goal.* Happiness must be our bridesmaid, not our bride. Many people make the great mistake of aiming directly at pleasure; they forget that pleasure comes only from the fulfillment of a duty or obedience to a law — for man is made to obey the laws of his own nature as inescapably as he must obey the law of gravity. A boy has pleasure eating ice-cream because he is fulfilling one of the "oughts" of human nature: eating. If he eats more ice-cream than the laws of his body sanction, he will no longer get the pleasure he seeks, but the pain of a stomachache. To seek pleasure, regardless of law, is to miss it.

Shall we start with pleasure or end with it? There are two answers to the question: the Christian and the pagan. The Christian says, "Begin with the fast and end with the feast, and you will really savor it." The pagan says, "Begin with the feast and end with the morning-after headache."

WORK

8

Work

VERY FEW PEOPLE IN THIS AGE do the kind of work they like to do. Instead of selecting their jobs by choice, they are forced by economic necessity to work at tasks which fail to satisfy them. Many of them say, "I ought to be doing something bigger," or "This job of mine is only important because I get paid." Such an attitude lies at the bottom of much unfinished and badly-executed work. The man who chooses his work because it fulfills a purpose he approves is the only one who grows in stature by working. He alone can properly say at the end of it, "It is finished!"

This sense of vocation is sadly lacking nowadays. The blame should not be placed on the complexity of our economic system, but on a collapse of our spiritual values. Any work, viewed in its proper perspective, can be used to ennoble us; but a necessary prelude to seeing this is to understand the philosophy of labor.

Every task we undertake has two aspects — *our purpose*, which makes us think it worth doing, and *the work itself*, regarded apart from its end-purpose. We play tennis to get exercise; but we play the game as well as possible, just for the joy of doing the thing well. The man who argued that he could get as much exercise by sloppy technique on the courts would have missed an understanding of the second aspect of all activity: the accomplishment of the task in accordance with its own standards of excellence. In the same way, a man working in an automobile factory may have, as his primary purpose, the earning of wages; but the purpose of the work itself is the excellent completion of the task. A workman should be aware of the second purpose at all times — as the artist is aware of the aim of beauty in his painting and the housewife is aware of the need for neatness when she dusts.

Today the first aspect of working has become paramount, and we tend to ignore the second… so that many workmen lead half-lives in their laboring hours. They are like gardeners, ordered to grow cabbage to give them sauerkraut juice, but indifferent as to whether their plots are weeded properly or their cabbages are healthy vegetables. This is a mistaken attitude: God Himself worked when He made the world and then, viewing it, He called it "good."

The legitimate pride in doing work well relieves it of much of its drudgery. Some people, who have held to this craftsman's standard, get a thrill from any job they do. They know the satisfaction of "a job well done" whether they are engaged in caning a chair or cleaning a horse's stall or carving a statue for a cathedral. Their honor and their self-respect are heightened by the discipline of careful work. They have retained the old attitude of the Middle Ages, when work was a sacred event, a ceremony, a source of spiritual merit. Labor was not then undertaken merely for the sake of economic gain, but was chosen through an inner compulsion, through a desire to project the creative power of God through our own human effort.

No task should be undertaken in a spirit which ignores either of these two primary aspects of work. To link together the two things — the joy of making a table well with the purpose of making it at all, which is to earn a living — the following principles should be kept in mind:

(1) *Work is a moral duty and not*, as many men imagine, *a mere physical necessity.* St. Paul said, "The man who refuses to work must be left to starve" (cf. 2 Th 3:10). When work is seen as a moral duty, it is apparent that it not only contributes to the social good, but also performs further services to the worker himself: it prevents the idleness from which many evils can arise and it also keeps his body in subjection to the reasoned will.

(2) *"To work is to pray."* The well-regulated life does not defer prayer until work has been accom-

plished; it turns the work itself into a prayer. We accomplish this when we turn to God at the beginning and completion of each task and mentally offer it up for love of Him. Then, whether we are nursing a child or making carburetors, turning a lathe or running an elevator, the task is sanctified. No amount of piety in leisure hours can compensate for slipshod labor on the job. But any honest task, well done, can be turned into a prayer.

(3) A medieval economist, Antonio of Florence, summed up the relationship of work to life in the happy formula: *"The object of making money is that we may provide for ourselves and our dependents. The object of providing for self and others is that one may live virtuously. The object of living virtuously is to save our souls and attain eternal happiness."*

Work should, in justice, receive two kinds of reward — for it is not only individual, but also social. John Jones, who works in a mine, is tired at the end of the day: this is his individual sacrifice. For it he receives his wages. But John Jones has also, during the day, made a social contribution to the economic well-being of the country and the world. For this social contribution, John Jones today is given nothing, even though he has a moral right to a share of the social wealth his work creates. We need a modification of the wage system, so that the worker may share in the profits, ownership or management of his industry. When labor leaders and capitalists thus agree together to give labor some capital to defend, there will no longer be two rival groups in industry; labor and management will become two cooperating members working together, as the two legs of a man cooperate to help him walk.

9

REPOSE

NEVER BEFORE HAVE MEN possessed so many time saving devices. Never before have they had so little time for leisure or repose. Yet few of them are aware of this: advertising has created in modern minds the false notion that leisure and not-working are the same — that the more we are surrounded by bolts and wheels, switches and gadgets, the more time we have conquered for our own.

But this division of our days into working and not-working is too simple; in practice, for most men, it leaves out the very possibility of real leisure. They waste precious hours away from work in aimless loafing, in negative waiting-around for something interesting to come along.

True repose is not a mere intermission between the acts of the working-life. It is an intense activity, but of a different kind. Just as sleeping is not a cessation of life, but living of a different sort from wakefulness, so repose is an activity no less creative than that of our working hours.

Repose — true leisure — cannot be enjoyed

without some recognition of the spiritual world, for the first purpose of repose is the contemplation of the good. Its goal is a true perspective one: the small incidents of everyday life in their relation to the larger goodness that surrounds us. Genesis tells us that after the creation of the world, *"God saw all that He had made, and found it very good"* (Gn 1:31). Such contemplation of his work is natural to man, whenever he, too, is engaged in a creative task. The painter stands back from his canvas to see whether the details of the seascape are properly placed. True repose is such a standing back to survey the activities that fill our days.

We cannot get a real satisfaction out of our work unless we pause, frequently, to ask ourselves why we are doing it, and whether its purpose is one our minds wholeheartedly approve. Perhaps one reason why so many of our economic and political projects miscarry is because they are in the hands of men with eyes so tightly glued to what they are doing that they never stop to question whether it should be done at all. Merely keeping busy, merely getting paid can never satisfy man's need for creative work.

A job of any kind can be lifted up and given Divine purpose, if it is seen in the perspective of Eternity. The sweeping of a floor, the driving of a garbage-truck, the checking of a list of boxcar numbers — all these can be "made good" through a simple act of the will which directs them to the service of God. The simplest task can be given spiritual significance and made Divine.

If we direct our work towards God, we shall work better than we know. The admission of this fact is another of the tasks for which we need repose. Once a week, man, reposing from work, does well to come before his God to admit how much of what he did during the week was the work of his Creator; he can remind himself, then, that the material on which he labored came from Other hands, that the ideas he employed entered his mind from a Higher source, that the very energy which he employed was a gift of God.

In such a mood of true repose, the scientist will see that he himself was not the author of his research volume on nature's laws, but only its proofreader. It was God who wrote the book. In such repose, the teacher will confess that every truth he passed on to his students was a ray from the sun of Divine Wisdom. The cook who peels potatoes after such a period of repose will handle them as humble gifts of God Himself.

Repose allows us to contemplate the little things we do in their relationship to the vast things which alone can give them worth and meaning. It reminds us that all actions get their worth from God: "worship" means admitting "worth." To worship is to restore to our workaday life its true worth by setting it in its real relationship to God, Who is its end and ours.

Such worship is a form of repose — of an intensely active and creative contemplation of Divine things, from which we arise refreshed. The promise of Jesus in the Gospel of St. Matthew is still waiting for those who are willing to hear it: *"Come to me, all you who labor and are burdened and I will give you rest"* (Mt 11:28).

10

THE IDLE IN THE MARKETPLACE

A GREAT AND DISTINGUISHED psychologist once said that the tragedy of man today was that he no longer believed he had a soul to save. To such a group Our Lord addressed His beautiful parable of the laborers in the vineyard (cf. Mt 20:1-16). Toward the close of the day the master of the vineyard went to the marketplace and said: "Why have you been standing here all the day idle?" In certain places of the East this custom still prevails — men gathering in front of mosques and public places with shovels in their hands, waiting to be hired.

This story has a spiritual application and refers to various kinds of idlers. In addition to those who idle in the literal sense, there are mere loafers with nothing to do. Many are idle in the sense of being industrious triflers, wearied with toils that accomplish no real worth. Many are idle because of constant indecision, and others become frustrated and worried, not knowing the purpose of life. To the human eye, there are not many idlers, but as the Eye of Heaven looks down to earth it must be like a vast marketplace wherein few labor. To the Divine, all such activity as the acquiring of wealth, marrying and giving in marriage, buying and selling, studying and painting, are all means to the supreme and final end which is the saving of one's soul. Every expenditure of human strength which makes what is a means an end, which isolates living from the goal of living, is a busy idleness, a sad and mournful unreality.

Despite this new and harsh definition of idleness which Our Divine Lord gives, there is nevertheless much hope in the story, for some were hired at the eleventh hour, and they received just as much as those who had labored all the day. It is never too late for God's grace. It is a peculiar psychological fact that those who turn to God late in life generally consider all their previous life wasted. St. Augustine reflecting on his wasted youth said: "Late have I loved You, O Beauty ever ancient, ever new. Late have I loved You." There are no hopeless cases; no life is too far spent to be recouped; no lifelong idleness precludes a few minutes of useful work in the vineyard of the Lord, even in the last few hours of life, as was the case with the penitent thief.

When the Lord gave everyone at the end of the day the same wages, those who had borne the heat and burdens of the sun complained that those who came in at the eleventh hour received just as much. To which Our Divine Lord retorted: "Does your eye see evil because I do good?" The thought of reward does not enter into the heavenly service. Those who lead a moral life for forty years and then protest the latecomers' salvation have the spirit of the hireling. With all the true acts of the spiritual man, the inspiration is love and not a desire of reward. One can not speak of the rewards of a true love in marriage without insulting the husband and wife. One can not associate compensation with the affection that twines a child's arms about a mother's neck, or that keeps her waiting in vigils that outwatch the patient stars. One cannot associate reward with the heroism of a man who would risk his life to save another. In like manner the servitors of daily piety and religion are as full of the charm and fascination and glory of self-forgetting devotion as any of these.

Physical idleness deteriorates the mind; spiritual idleness deteriorates the heart. The joint action of air and water can turn an iron bar to rust. Therefore at every hour in the marketplace, man must ask himself: "Why am I standing here idle?"

LOVE

11

THE THREE CAUSES OF LOVE

E VERY LOVE RESTS ON A TRIPOD. Every love has three
bases or supports: goodness, knowledge and
similarity.

Take *goodness* first: a man may be mistaken in
his choice of what seems to him to be good, but he
can never desire anything unless he believes in its
intrinsic goodness. The prodigal son was seeking
something good for himself — something to satisfy
his hunger — when he tried to live on husks; he was
wrong only in his judgment, in thinking husks as
food for a man. All of us are in the same predicament
as he. We are forever trying to fill our lives, our
minds, our bodies, our homes with "goods," and we
accept nothing unless it seems, at the moment, to
have some good in it. But our estimates are not
always correct; we may mistake an apparent for a
real good, thus injuring ourselves.

Without this reaching-out towards goodness,
there would be no love: neither love of country, nor
of pleasures, of friend, nor of spouse. Through
loving, each heart tries to acquire a perfection which

it lacks, or to express the perfection it already owns. All love springs out of goodness, for goodness, by its nature, is lovable to man.

The goodness which we love in other people is not always a moral goodness; it may be physical goodness, or utilitarian goodness. In such cases, an individual is loved because of the pleasure that he gives us, or because he is useful to us, or because he can "get it for us wholesale," or for some other reason in which selfishness is involved. But even then, there is a good we seek in our loving and unless something somehow seems good to us, we simply cannot care for it.

But *knowledge* is also involved in every love: We cannot love what we do not know. "Introduce me to her," is the phrase of a man who seeks the knowledge of a woman which, he recognizes, must precede the possibility of his really loving her. Even the "dream girl" of the bachelor has to be built up from fragments of knowledge in his mind. Hatred comes from want of knowledge, as love comes from knowledge; thus, bigotry is properly related to ignorance.

Knowledge, in the early stages, is a condition of love; but as the relationship deepens, love increases knowledge. A wife and husband who have lived together many years possess a new kind of knowledge of each other, deeper than any spoken word or any analysis of motives could provide. This knowledge (impossible in the honeymoon weeks) comes gradually from love-in-action, as a kind of intuitional understanding of what lies in the mind and heart of the other. It is thus possible for us to love beyond our knowledge, to allow faith to fill up the insufficiency of our intellectual understanding. A simple person in good faith may therefore have a greater love of God than a theologian, and this love can give him a keener understanding of the ways of God with human hearts than any psychologist will possess.

One of the reasons why decent people shrink from vulgar discussions of sex is that the knowledge two people gain of one another in so intimate a relationship is, by its very nature, incommunicable to others. The whole exchange is so personal that those involved shrink from sharing it with outsiders — the knowledge thus gained is too sacred to be profaned. And it is a psychological fact that those whose theoretical knowledge of sex has been realized in the unifying love of marriage are least inclined to bring the matter out of its twilit realm of shared mystery to the glaring light of public discussion. This is not at all because they are "disillusioned" about sex, but because sex has now been changed by the transcendent alchemy of love, so that its nature can no longer be understood by those who stand outside the shared experience. On the other hand, those whose knowledge of sex has not been sublimated into the mystery of love (and who are therefore frustrated) are the ones who like to talk about sex. Husbands and wives whose marriages are marred by infidelity seek such discussions; fathers and mothers who are happy in their relationship never want to mention it.

When knowledge has been transmuted to love, it fills the heart so full that no outsider could contribute anything further, and the matter need never be aired. People who talk about their intimate relations confess, by doing so, that they have not raised their love high enough to turn it into a mystery, or transformed it into the only kind of love between the sexes that deserves the name.

The third leg of the tripod on which love rests is *similarity*: similarity between two persons, leading to love, need not indicate that they are both alike in actual fact. It can mean merely that one possesses in actuality what the other owns potentially. Because the human heart, itself imperfect, desires perfection, we seek, through love, to make up for our own deficiencies. The homely young man will wish to marry a beautiful girl: the potential beauty (which he does not possess himself, but for which he has a hunger) attracts him to that which is beautiful beyond himself.

Similarity underlies even the most vulgar and tawdry of our loves. The woman who is a social climber cultivates "important" people because they possess, in actuality, what she would like to have, but lacks. On a much higher level, saints love sinners — not because they share developed qualities of soul, but because the saint is able to apprehend the possible virtue in the sinner. It was thus that the Son of God Himself became the Son of man: He loved what man might be and, in the words of St. Augustine, "He became man that man might become like God."

12

WHEN LOVERS FAIL THERE IS LOVE

MARRIAGES FAIL WHEN LOVE is regarded not as something transparent like a window pane which looks out on the heavens, but as something opaque like a curtain which sees nothing beyond the human. When couples do not see that the love of the flesh is the preface to the love of the spirit, one of the partners is often made the object of worship in place of God. This is the essence of idolatry, the worship of the image of the reality; the mistaking of the copy for the original, and the frame for the picture.

Human love promises something only God can give. When God is ignored in love, the one who was worshipped as a deity is discovered not to be a god, or even an angel. Because he or she did not give all that was promised, being incapable of giving it, because not Divine, the other feels betrayed, deceived, disappointed and cheated. The stem of the rose is blamed for not bearing what it could not bear, the marble bust of deity. The result is that erotic love turns to hate when the other is discovered to have feet of clay — to be a woman instead of an angel, to be a man instead of an Apollo. When the ecstasy does not continue, and the band stops playing, and the champagne of life loses its sparkle, the other partner is called a cheat and a robber — and then finally called to a divorce court on the grounds of incompatibility.

Then begins the search for a new partner, on the assumption that some other human being can supply what only God can give. Instead of seeing that the basic reason for the failure of the marriage was the refusal to use married love as the vestibule of the Divine, one thinks that husks can satisfy, when one was meant to eat only the bread of angels. The very fact that a man or a woman seeks a new partner is a proof that there never was any love at all, for though sex is replaceable, love is not. Sex is for a pleasure; love is for a person.

Cows can graze on other pastures, but a person admits of no substitution. As soon as a person becomes equated with a package to be judged only by its wrappings, it will not be long when the tinsel turns green and the package will be discarded. This arrangement enslaves a woman, because she is much more a creature of time than man, and her security becomes less and less through the years. She is always much more concerned about her age than a man, and thinks more of marriage in terms of time. This is because a man is afraid of dying before he has lived, but a woman is basically afraid of dying before she has begotten life. A woman wants the fulfillment of life more than a man, and it is less the experience of life that she craves, than the prolongation of life. Whenever the laws and the customs of a country permit an arrangement whereby a woman can be discarded because she has dishpan hands, it ends by making her the slave not of dishpans but of man.

Life is not a snare nor an illusion. It would be that only if there were no Infinite to satisfy our yearnings. Everyone wants a Love that will never die and one that has no moments of hate or satiety. That Love lies beyond humans.

Human love is a spark from the great flame of Eternity. The happiness which comes from the unity of two in one flesh is a prelude to that greater communion of two in one spirit. In this way, marriage becomes a tuning fork to the song of the angels, or a river that runs to the sea. Then it is evident that there is an answer to the elusive mystery of love and that somewhere there is a reconciliation of the quest and the goal, and that is in final union with God, where the chase and the capture, the romance and the marriage fuse into one. For since God is boundless, eternal Love, it will take an ecstatic eternal chase to sound its depths.

13

True Love

THERE ARE TWO KINDS OF LOVE: love for its own
pleasure, or love for the sake of another; the first
is carnal love, the second is spiritual. Carnal love
knows the other person only in a biological moment. Spiritual love knows the other person at all
moments. In erotic love, the burdens of the other are
regarded as impairing one's own happiness; in spiritual love, the burdens of others are opportunities for
service.

Somewhere along the line, the modern world
has been duped and fooled into giving the name of
love to some vague obsession which parades itself in
every billboard advertisement, reigns in the film
industry, puzzles dramatists who must solve tri-
angles short of suicide, makes novels best-sellers,
perfumes so exotic as to be unfit for a tyro's
concupiscence, and humor more spicy. Love has
become so vulgarized, so carnalized, that those who
really love are almost afraid to use the word. It is
used now almost exclusively to describe one of the
opposite sex, rather than a person; it is made to

revolve around glands, rather than a will, and is centered in biology instead of personality. Even when it disguises itself as infatuation for another, it is nothing else than a desire to intensify its own self-centeredness.

Purely human love is the embryo of the Love of the Divine. One finds some suggestions of this in Plato, who argues that the purpose of love is to make the first step toward religion. He pictures love for beautiful persons being transformed into love for beautiful souls, then into a love of justice, goodness and finally God Who is their source. Erotic love is, therefore, a bridge which one crosses, not a buttress where one sits and rests; it is not an airport but an airplane; it is always going somewhere else, upwards and onwards. All carnal love presupposes incompleteness, deficiency, yearning for completion, and an attraction for enrichment, for all love is a flight for immortality. There is a suggestion of Divine Love in every form of erotic love, as the lake reflects the moon. The only reason there is love for creatures in human hearts, is that it may lead to the love of the Creator. As food is for the body, as the body is for the soul, as the material is for the spiritual, so the flesh is for the eternal. That is why in the language of human love, there can often be detected the language of Divinity, such as "worship," "angel," "adore."

The Savior did not crush and then extinguish the flames that burned in Magdalene's heart, but transfigured them to a new object of affection. The Divine commendation that was given to the woman who poured out the ointment on the feet of her Savior, reminded her that love which once sought its own pleasure can be transmuted into a love that will die for the beloved. For that reason He referred to His burial at the very moment her thoughts were closest to life.

Because it is in the Divine plan to use the love of the flesh as a stepping stone to the love of the Divine, it always happens in a well-regulated moral heart, that as time goes on, the erotic love diminishes, and the religious love increases. That is why in true marriages the love of God increases through the years, not in the sense that husband and wife love one another less, but that they love God more. Love passes from an affection for outer appearances, to those inner depths of personality which embody the Divine Spirit.

There are few things more beautiful in life than to see that deep passion of man for woman which begot children as the mutual incarnation of their love, transfigured into that deeper "passionless passion and wild tranquility" which is God.

14

The Effects of Want of Love

MOST PEOPLE IN THE WORLD are unloved. Some do not make themselves lovable because of their selfishness; others do not have enough Christian spirit to love those who do not love them. The result is that the world is full of lonely hearts. Here we speak not of love in the romantic or carnal sense, but in the higher sense of generosity, forgiveness, kindness and sacrifice. Perhaps it would help some to know some of the psychological effects of not loving others in a really noble and unselfish way.

The first effect of not receiving love because one is generous and loving toward others is cynicism and even hostility. Never a good word can be said for anyone. Because one is unloved one tries to make everyone else unlovable. Characters are assassinated, the noblest motives reduced to the basest, and slanders believed and propagated. When others do show them kindness they look "for the catch in it"; even gifts are viewed with suspicion and the sincerest of compliments acknowledged with a charge of insincerity. Because such egotists are so miserable they seek to make everyone else miserable. Never once do they see that they are the cause of their own unhappiness. Someone else is always to blame. "I bumped into the other car, because you made me nervous this morning at breakfast by asking about my bank balance." "I have a cold now because you did not give me a mink coat like the wives of the other officials have."

And the effect of want of love is the martyrdom complex, which is a morbid attempt to get pity or sympathy when real love is gone. Feigning sickness is one of the tricks. Because good health does not win the affection of others, one pretends to be wounded in the firm hope that someone else will bind the wounds. The "pain" which is in the mind is loss of love. That "pain" is translated into the body and becomes sickness. If one could put into words what goes on inside of such a person it might be this: "I really want to be well. But if I become sick, then others *must* love me." Just as headaches can be caused by a desire to escape responsibility, so disease can be caused by a desire to win affection. This reaches a point in some where they become bedridden for years or unable to walk. In the San Francisco earthquake it was said that over thirty people who had not walked in over a period of twenty years, got up and walked. These were mental, not physical cripples.

Another type of reaction is in those who admit

that they need love, but say: "I will pretend from now on that I do not need it." As a result they develop a false spirit of independence, become quarrelsome, oppose every idea and suggestion regardless of how good it is, develop anti-social instincts, smoke in front of no-smoking signs, and park in front of no-parking signs. Hardness and roughness and a certain toughness and boorishness of character is many times nothing other than a bold front for want of love.

It is very likely that the overemphasis on security in society today is due to a want of love. In other generations people wanted to be happy, and many of them were happy in the framework both of a family and of a permanent marriage bond, or in the embrace of religion. Now the instability of the home through divorce is increasing. A substitute must be found for married love, and it comes out in a ruthless quest for power and security which is only one of the lesser ingredients of happiness. The business man who is completely lost in his business and stays at the office late hours rather than go home may sometimes be doing that to compensate for his want of love at home. Some doctors are now tracing some skin diseases to mental causes. It has been said that some people who are afraid to "face the world" develop skin blemishes. A "stained mind" becomes a "stained body." Whatever be the medical evidence to support this view, it is true that no group of women seem to have complexions like nuns. Most nuns never look into a mirror, but they have one incomparably fine beauty aid which many other people lack, namely, a good conscience and peace of soul. The skin of those who suffer with a hidden sense of guilt almost tells the story of the diseases going on inside the soul. One person who had repressed guilt and kept saying to herself: "I am a moral leper," developed a skin infection which vanished when reconciliation was made with her husband.

There is no cure for want of love but love. There will always be love for the lovable, but there will never be love for the unlovable unless we begin to love them for God's sake. Thus we are brought back again to religion and to God Whose New Testament definition of His essence is: "God is love" (1 Jn 4:8).

15

Reflections on Love

THE EGO HAS A PECULIAR WAY of disguising the real reasons for its love. It can pretend to be interested in another's welfare while actually it is seeking its own pleasure.

There are some people who love to boast of their tolerance, but actually it is inspired by egotism; they want to be left alone in their own ideas, however wrong they be, so they plead for a tolerance of other people's ideas. But this kind of tolerance is very dangerous, for it becomes intolerance as soon as the ego is disturbed or menaced. That is why a civilization which is tolerant about false ideas instead of being charitable to persons is on the eve of a great wave of intolerance and persecution.

The egotist always considers his ego in terms of not having or wanting something. His principal action is drawing something to himself like the mouth which absorbs food. There is no outgoing, no service, and never a sacrifice, because he interprets sacrifice as the diminishing of himself.

True love, on the contrary, feels that the need

to give is more imperious than the need to receive. At the beginning of love there is a feeling that one can never give enough. Regardless of how precious the gift, it still seems to fall short of what one would offer. Price tags are torn off, because we want no proportion established between the gift and the need of giving. The tragedy of love when it begins to die, is that then people do not even give what they have. No longer is there a question of not being able to give enough; there is rather no giving at all.

In real love there is pity and need. Pity in the sense that one feels the need of expansion and of giving to the point of exhaustion; need, because of a void that one would see filled. True love receives without ever interpreting what is given. It never seeks another motive than that of love itself. He who asks "why" something is given does not trust.

One of the tragedies of our time is that freedom is interpreted in terms of freedom *from* something instead of in terms of love. The man who loves everybody is the free man; the man who hates is the man who has already enslaved himself. The man who hates is dependent on that which he cannot love — and therefore he is not free. To hate one's next door neighbor is a restriction of freedom. It demands walking around the block so one will not see him, or waiting until he leaves the house before leaving oneself.

It is our loves and desires that determine our

pains. If our supreme love is the pleasure of the body, then our greatest pain is loss of health; if our supreme love is wealth, then our deepest worry is insecurity; if our supreme love is God, then our greatest fear is sin.

The great mystery is not why we love, but why we are loved. It is easy to understand why we love because of our incompleteness and our radical dissatisfaction apart from goodness. But why anyone should love us is the mystery, for we know when we look at our real selves how very little there is to love. Why creatures should love us is not too great a mystery, for they are imperfect too. But for God to love us — that we will never understand. The soul that has finally come to love God is worried by the thought that he has already lost so much time. As St. Augustine said: "Late have I loved You, O Beauty ever ancient, ever new. Late have I loved You." But, on the other hand, this regret is compensated for by the knowledge that it was always in the Divine plan that we should eventually come to know God.

We love to see ourselves idealized in the minds of others. That is one of the beautiful joys of love. We become fresh, innocent, brave, strong in the mind of the beloved. Love covers up the corruption of the soul. The winter of discontent is forgotten by being clothed in the blossoms of a new spring. After a while the lover begins to substitute what he really is in his own mind, with what he is in the mind of the other. It is this idealization which pleases in love. That is why love gives an incentive to betterment. When the other thinks well of us, we try to be worthy of that opinion. The fact that others assume us to be good is a great incentive to goodness. That is why, too, one of the basic principles of life ought to be to assume goodness in others; thus we make them good.

16

The Mystery of Love

THERE COMES A MOMENT in even the noblest of human loves when the mystery has gone. As jewelers may casually handle the most precious stones without troubling to admire them, one has now grown "used to" the best, and has come to take it for granted. What we completely possess, we can no longer desire. What we have already attained, we cannot hope for. Yet hope and desire and, above all, mystery, are needed to keep our interest in life alive.

When wonder has vanished from our days, then they become banal. Our minds were made to function at the stretch and to reach out, forever, towards the solution of some lofty problem that forever eludes us. It is possible that the popularity of mystery novels in our day is occasioned by the fact that so many people have ceased to dwell on the mysteries of faith and are looking, in any cheap substitute that comes to hand, for something to replace what they have lost. Readers of mystery stories spend all their wonder on the method by which someone was killed; they do not, as the contemporaries of Dante and of Michelangelo would have done, wonder about the eternal fate of those who die.

Man cannot be happy if he is satiated; our zest comes from the fact that there are doors not yet opened, veils not yet lifted, notes that have not been struck. If a "love" is only physical, marriage will bring the romance to an end: the chase is ended, and the mystery is solved. Whenever any person is thus taken for granted, there is a loss of the sensitivity and delicacy which are the essential condition of friendship, joy and love in human relations. Marriage is no exception; one of its most tragic outcomes is mere possession without desire.

There is no love left when one hits bottom, or imagines that he has; the personality we have exhausted of its mystery is a bore. There must be always something unrevealed, some mystery we have not probed, some passion that we cannot glut — and this is true even in the arts. We do not want to hear a singer constantly reiterate her highest note, nor have an orator tear a passion to tatters.

In a true marriage there is an ever-deepening mystery and, therefore, an ever-enchanting romance. At least four of the mysteries of marriage can be tabulated. First comes the mystery of the other partner's physical being, the mystery of sex. When that mystery has been solved, and the first baby is born, a new mystery begins: the husband sees in his wife a thing he never saw before — the beautiful mystery of motherhood. She sees in him the sweet mystery of fatherhood. As other children come to revive their strength and beauty, the husband never seems older to his wife than on the day they met, and the wife appears to him as freshly beautiful as when they first became engaged.

When the children reach the age of reason, a third mystery unfolds: that of mothercraft and fathercraft — the disciplining of young minds and hearts in the ways of God. As the children grow to maturity this mystery continues to deepen; each child's personality is something for the parents to explore and then to form closer to the likeness of the God of love.

The fourth mystery of the happily married involves their social living, the contribution that they jointly make to the well-being of the world. Here lies the root of democracy, for in the family the individual is not valued for what he is worth, nor for what he can do, but for what he is. His status, his position in the home, is granted him by virtue of merely being alive. If a child is dumb or blind, if a son has been maimed at the war, he is still loved for himself and for his intrinsic worth as a child of God. No parent mitigates his love because of changes in a child's earning power or worldly wisdom, or troubles about the class to which his offspring may belong. This reverence for personality for its own sake in the family is the social principle on which the wider life of the community depends and is a potent reminder of the most important of all political principles: the state exists for the person, and not the person for the state.

17

LOVE AND ECSTASY

ECSTASY MEANS TO BE "carried out of oneself" and, broadly speaking, the very fact of loving carries the lover out of himself by leading him to center his thoughts, beyond himself, on the beloved. Adolescent boys and girls are often surprised to find that their elders know they have fallen in love; they give themselves away by their dreamy inattention, by staring into space and by indifference to such things as mealtimes. Love has "carried them away."

Love, again, is at the bottom of all the stories about the absent-minded professors who, on rainy nights, put the umbrella to bed and stand themselves in the sink; the things of the mind they love have "carried them out" of their surroundings. Any great love has a similar effect: it makes the lover indifferent to physical hardships and sordid surroundings. The hovel of a man and wife who love each other is a far more joyous place than the rich apartment of the couple who have lost their love. Love of God begets an even greater indifference to our environment: a saint like St. Vincent de Paul was so carried away by his love for God's poor that he forgot to feed himself. As Edna St. Vincent Millay wrote of the Christian life: "If you pitch your tent each evening nearer the town of your true desire, and glimpse its gates less far, then you lay you down on nettles, you lay you down with vipers, and you scarcely notice where you are."

But there is one great difference between human love and the love of God, although both of them "carry us away." In human love, the ecstasy comes at the beginning. But when it is a matter of loving God, the ecstasy is attained only after one has passed through much suffering and agony of soul. In bodily enjoyments, we encounter first the feast and then the fast, and maybe the headache as well. But the spirit encounters first the fast, and perhaps the headache, only as a necessary prelude to the feast. The ecstatic pleasures enjoyed by a young husband and wife at the commencement of their marriage are, in a sense, a "bait," inducing them to fulfill their mission of parenthood. The honeymoon is a kind of Divine credit extended to those who, later on, will have to pay the costs of rearing a family. But no great ecstasy, either of the spirit or of the flesh, is given us as a permanent possession without our having to pay for it. Every ecstasy carries a price tag with it.

"First fervor is false fervor" in marriage as in religion. The earliest ecstasy is not the true, lasting love we seek to find and hold. That may come to us

— but only after many purging trials, fidelities under stress, perseverance through discouragement and a steady pursuit of our Divine destiny past all the allurements of this earth. The deep, ecstatic love of some Christian fathers and mothers is a beautiful thing to see: but they have won it after passing through their Calvaries. Theirs is the true ecstasy, which belongs less to youth than to old age.

The first ecstasy of love is a thrill, but a somewhat selfish thrill: in it, the lover seeks to get from the beloved all that she will give. In the second ecstasy, he tries to receive from God all that both of them can give. If love is identified with the early ecstasy alone, it will seek its prolongation in another person's presence; if it is identified with a unifying, enduring and eternal love, it will seek the deepening of its mystery in the Divine, Who put all loves into our hearts.

Too many husbands and wives expect their partners in marriage to give what only God can give: eternal ecstasy. Yet if any man or woman could do that, he would be God. We are right to want the ecstasy of love; but if we expect to enjoy it through the flesh, which is merely on pilgrimage to God, we prepare ourselves for disappointment. The first ecstasy of love is not an illusion; but it is only a kind of travel folder, a foretaste, a preview, urging body and soul to start the journey towards eternal joys. If the first ecstasy passes, this change is not an invitation to

love another person, but to love in another way —
and the other way is Christ's way, the way of Him
Who said: "I *am* the Way."

CHILDREN

18

MOTHERHOOD

HUMAN MOTHERHOOD IS twofold in its essence, and is a more complex thing than motherhood among the animals. There is, first, the physical act of giving birth, which women share with all of nature. As the tree bears fruit and the hen hatches her eggs, so every mother, by the act of birth, is bound up with the life of all living things, and of her it may be rightly said, "Blessed is the fruit of thy womb."

But human motherhood has a second and far lordlier aspect — that of the spirit. The soul of a child does not emanate from the mother's soul or body, but is freshly created by God Himself, Who infuses it into the body of the unborn child. Physiological motherhood is glorified by this cooperation with God Himself, Who fathered the baby's soul and then permitted a woman to clothe it in her flesh. The human mother does not bear a mere animal but a *human being*, made to the image and likeness of the God Who created it.

Every child born of woman has, then, two fathers: his earthly father, without whom he could not have life, and his Heavenly Father, without Whom he could not possess a personality, a soul, an irreplaceable "I." The mother is the essential partner through whom both fathers work. Her own relationship to the child has two resulting aspects: there is the mother-baby aspect, wherein the child is physically and almost absolutely dependent on the mother. But there is also the mother-person relationship (expressed at baptism, when the child is given its own name). This confirms the dignity and separate selfhood of even the smallest infant and foreshadows his right eventually to lead his own life and to depart from his parents to cling to a wife of his own.

Every birth requires a submission and a disciplining. The earth itself must undergo harrowing before it passively accepts the seed. In woman, the submission is not passive: it is sacrificial, consciously creative, and for this selflessness her whole nature has been formed. It is well known that women are capable of far more sustained sacrifice than men; a man may be a hero in a crisis, and then slip back to mediocrity. He lacks the moral endurance which enables a woman to be heroic through the years, months, days and even seconds of her life, when the very repetitive monotony of her tasks wears down the spirit. Not only a woman's days, but her nights — not only her mind, but her body must share in the Calvary of motherhood. That is why women have a surer understanding of the doctrine of redemption than men have: they have come to associate the risk of death with life in childbirth, and to understand the sacrifice of self to another through the many months preceding it.

In a mother two of the great spiritual laws are united into one: love of neighbor and cooperation with God's grace — and both of them are applied in a unique way. For love of neighbor, to anyone except a mother, is love of a non-self; a mother's neighbor during pregnancy is one with herself, yet to be loved differently from the self. The sacrifice sometimes involved in neighborly love now takes place within her flesh: the agent and the object of her sacrifice are both contained within her.

And the cooperation with grace in a mother, although it may be unconscious on her part, yet makes her a partner of Divinity: every human mother is, in a sense, "overshadowed by the Holy Spirit." Not a priest, and yet endowed with a kind of priestly power, she, too, brings God to man, and man to God. She brings God to man by accepting her mother's role, thus permitting God to infuse a new soul into her body for it to bear. She brings man to God in childbirth itself, when she allows herself to be used as an instrument by which another child of God is born into the world.

If motherhood is seen as a matter involving only a woman and a man it is seen too astigmatically, and without the honor that is its due. For to comprehend the real significance of motherhood, we must include the spiritual element that goes to make a child — we must see the human woman cooperating with her husband, the father of the human baby, and with God, the Father of a soul that is eternal, indestructible and unlike any other ever formed throughout the history of the world. Thus every human motherhood involves a partnership with the Divine.

19

Parents and Children

THERE ARE NO JUVENILE delinquents; there are only delinquent parents. The Fourth Commandment, "Honor thy father and thy mother," is hardly ever quoted today as the means of restoring domestic peace. If discipline in the home is neglected, it is rarely made up for later. As Coleridge said: "If you bring up your children in a way which puts them out of sympathy with the religious feelings of the nations in which they live, the chances are that they will ultimately turn out ruffians and fanatics, and one as likely as the other." The effects of the conduct of children on their parents vary. Mothers suffer more at their evil ways than fathers enjoy their good ways.

The duty of parents to children is to rule while avoiding exasperating severity on the one hand and excessive indulgences on the other. God gives parents a child as so much plastic material that can be molded for good or evil. What if God placed a precious diamond in the hands of parents and told them to inscribe on it a sentence which would be read on the Last Day, and shown as an index of their thoughts and ideals? What caution they would exercise in their selection! And yet the example parents give their children will be that by which they will be judged on the Last Day. This tremendous responsibility never means that parents, when their children do wrong, should provoke them to wrath, for wrath leads to discouragement. Parents hold the place of God in the house. If they act as tyrants they will develop unconsciously anti-religious sentiments in their children. Children love approbation and can be easily cast down into despair when blamed excessively for trivial faults. With great difficulty can children ever be taught the Love and Mercy of God, if His vice-regents in the home act without it and are so difficult to please. When good intentions are rated low, and children are put under the ban of dishonor, they are likely to show they are no better than their parents think they are.

Children came into their own with Christianity when its Divine Founder said: "Suffer the little children to come unto Me, and forbid them not, for of such is the Kingdom of Heaven." He consecrated childhood by becoming a child, playing on the green hills of Nazareth and watching the mother eagles stir among their young. From that day it became eternally true: "Train a boy in the way he should go; and when he is old he will not depart from it" (Pr 22:6). As the twig is bent, so is the tree. It is interesting, when one sees children, to speculate from the way they act as to the kind of homes from which they come. As one can judge the vitality of a tree from the fruit it produces, so one can tell the character of the parents from their children. One knows that from certain homes there will never be an errant child, while a glance at a mother or father will reveal a future full of fears for the child.

The present tendency is to shift responsibility to the school. But it must be remembered that education will make as much difference to a child as soil and air and sunshine do. A seed will grow better in one soil and climate than in another, but the kind of tree that grows depends on the kind of seed that is sowed. Then too, one must inquire if education is of the mind alone, or also of the will. Knowledge is in the mind; character is in the will. To pour knowledge into the mind of a child, without disciplining his will to goodness, is like putting a rifle into the hands of a child. Without education of the mind a child could be a stupid devil. With education of the mind, but without love of goodness, a child could grow up to be a clever devil.

The nation of tomorrow is the youth of today. They are the assurance of progress; the fresh arrows to a better future; the wings of aspiration. Even in war the strength of a nation is not in its bombs, but in the soldiers who defend it. In peace, it is not economics or politics that save, but good economists and good politicians — but to be that, they must be good children. To be that, there must in the first place be the grace of God; in the second place, in the home lessons of love and truth; in the schools, knowledge and self-control. Even in their early failures, the parents are not to be discouraged, remembering that fifteen centuries ago when the heart of a mother was broken for her wanton boy, St. Ambrose said to her: "Fear not, Monica; the child of so many tears cannot perish." That vain and wanton boy grew up to be the great and learned St. Augustine, whose *Confessions* everyone ought to read before he dies.

YOUTH

20

Blood, Sweat and Tears

Recently a woman at a Forum asked an important politician this question: "Why is it that our political leaders never speak of blood, sweat, tears and sacrifice, but only of how much they will give the farmers and the manufacturers and the labor unions if they are elected?" The politician answering quoted another politician, but it seemed as if he missed the deep significance of the woman's question. Actually, she was a spokesman of a large segment of the American people who know enough about history and psychology to know that no nation, as no individual, ever achieves anything worth while except through sacrifice and self-denial.

Toynbee pointed out that sixteen out of nineteen civilizations which have decayed from the beginning of history to the present, have rotted from within; only three fell to attacks from without. Very often an attack from the outside solidifies a nation and strengthens its moral fiber. Lincoln once said he never feared that America would be conquered from without, but that it might fall from within. Lenin once said that America would collapse by spending itself to death, an eventuality that is not too distant with a national debt of a little less than three hundred billion dollars.

Was Walter Whitman speaking of our age as well as his own when he wrote: "Society in these days is cankered, crude, superstitious and rotten… Genuine belief seems to have left us.… The great cities reek with respectable as well as non-respectable robbery and scoundrels. In fashionable life, flippancy, tepid amours, weak infidelities, small aims, or no aims at all, only to kill time.… It is as if we were somehow endowed with a vast and thoroughly appointed body, but then left with little or no soul."

Whitman's worry was in the woman's mind for she was disturbed about our indifference, tepidity and moral apathy. If there is anything that is becoming clear in our national life, it is that so-called progressive education is extremely unprogressive. Juvenile delinquency, crime, racketeering, political scandals—all these illegitimate children are dropped on the doorstep of an educational theory that denied a distinction between right and wrong and assumed that self-restraint was identical with the destruction of personality. Every instinct and impulse in either a child or an adult, does not, if left to itself, necessarily produce good results. Man has a hunting instinct which is good when directed to deer in season, but bad when directed to the police in season or out of season. The disrespect for authority which is the outgrowth of the stupidity that every individual is his own determinant of right and wrong has now become an epidemic of lawlessness.

Someday our educators will awaken to several basic facts about youth: (1) Youth has an intellect and a will. The intellect is the source of his knowledge; the will, the source of his decisions. If his choices are wrong, the youth will be wrong regardless of how much he knows. (2) Education through the communication of knowledge does not necessarily make a good man; it can conceivably make learned devils instead of stupid devils. (3) Education is successful when it trains the mind to see the right targets, and disciplines the will to choose them rather than the wrong targets.

At present two currents manifest themselves in our American way of life: one is in the direction of a great development of moral character both in individuals and in the nation; the other is toward the surrender of morality and responsibility through a socialist state in which there will be no morality but state-morality, no conscience but state-conscience. Of the two the first is by far the stronger, though neither politics nor economics has seen it. Some of our educators are turning away from the spoiled child psychology, in which the child was called progressive if he did whatever he wanted; now the return is toward doing a little bit of thinking and working in order to wrest us out of our juvenile delinquency and moral flabbiness.

Youth particularly is yearning for something hard; it no longer believes its teachers who say that good or evil is a point of view and it makes no difference in which you believe. They now want to believe that something is so evil that we ought to fight against it, and something is so good that we ought, if necessary, to steel and discipline ourselves and even die to defend it. This latent power of blood and sweat and tears in our American youth will be captured within the next generation by one of the other forces: either by some political crackpot who will turn that desire for sacrifice into something like Nazism, Fascism or Communism, or by our leaders, political, educational and moral who will first show self-discipline and moral courage in their own lives and thus give an example to others.

The greatest responsibility falls on religious leaders whose message ought to be the message the woman wanted from politicians — the clarion call to restraint on evil influences and the showing forth of altruism and love of God.

21

TEENAGERS

ADOLESCENCE, OR "TEENAGE," IS the short hour between the springtime and the summer of life. Before the teenage is reached, there is very little individuality or personality, but as soon as the teens begin, the emotional life takes on the character of its environment, like water takes its shape from the vessel into which it is poured. The adolescent begins to be conscious of himself and others, and for that reason begins to live in solitude. The youth is more lonely than many parents and teachers know; perhaps the teenager agonizes in a greater solitariness of spirit than at any other time in life until maturity when the sense of unrequited guilt begins to weigh down the human soul.

As the teenager projects his personality to the world round about him, he seems to get further away from it. Between his soul and the world there seems to be a wall. There is never a complete self analysis. As it takes an infant a long time to coordinate his eyes and his hands, so it takes the teenager a long time to adjust himself completely to this great broad world to which he feels so strangely related. He cannot yet take it in stride; novelty, new emotional experiences, great dreams and hopes flood his soul, each demanding attention and satisfaction. He does not confide his emotional states to others; he just lives. It is hard for the adult to penetrate the shell into which the teenager crawls. Like Adam after his fall, he hides from discovery.

Along with this loneliness, there goes a great desire to be noticed, for egotism is a vice that has to be mastered early in youth. This craving for attention accounts for the loudness in manner of some teenagers. Not only does it attract the gaze of others, but it also experiences a latent sense of rebellion against others, and affirms that he is living for himself in his own way and as he pleases.

Along with this quality of impenetrability the teenager becomes an imitator. Being in rebellion against the fixed and being governed largely by fleeting impressions, he becomes like a chameleon, which takes on the colors of the objects upon which it is placed. He becomes a hero or a bandit, a saint or a thief, depending on the environment or his reading or his companions. This spirit of imitation reveals itself in the dress. Overalls, shirts sticking out of trousers and overhanging like the flag of a defeated army, hair cuts fashioned after the savages of Oceania — all these become universal among young people who are afraid to march "against the grain."

There are few natural leaders among teenagers, most of them being content to follow others. In this unconscious mimicry of others is a moral danger, for character is dependent on the ability to say "No". Unless education can give to teenagers a training of the will, many of them will slip into adulthood and become slaves of propaganda and public opinion the rest of their lives. Instead of creating, they imitate. To create is to recognize the spirit in things; to imitate is to submerge personality at the lowest level of the mass.

Elders must not be too critical of the teenagers, particularly when they rebel against them. From one point of view they are not in rebellion against restraint, but against their elders for not giving them a goal and purpose of life. The teenager's protest is not conscious. He does not know why he hates his parents, why he is rebellious against authority, why his fellow teenagers are becoming more and more delinquent. But the real reason is under the surface; it is an unconscious protest against a society which has not given him a pattern of life. The schools he attends have never stressed restraint, discipline or self-control. Many of the teachers have defined freedom and even democracy as the right to do whatever you please. When this temporary phase of rebellion is past, the teenagers will look for some great cause to which they can make a total dedication. They must have an ideal. In many instances today, they have no greater object of worship than to wrap their emotional lives around a movie hero, a movie star, a band leader or a crooner. This sign of decaying civilizations will pass when the catastrophe comes. Then youth will look for a different type to imitate, namely, either heroes or saints. A sad commentary it is on our civilization that the teenagers have never rallied around heroes. This is because they are not yet ready for the more solid ideal. But it will come. And when it does, education must be careful lest in reacting against "progressive" education devoid of discipline, they follow false sacrificial gods. The latent capacity for doing the brave and heroic which is in every youth will soon come to the surface, and when it does, please God, it will be both for heroes and saints that they center their affection. The ascetic ideal has passed away from the elders, but God sends fresh generations into the world to give the world a fresh start. Our teenagers will one day find their right ideals, in love of God and love of country, and particularly the former, for it is the function of religion to make possible to men sacrifices which in the face of reason or egotism would never come to the surface.

22

More About Teenagers

What Americans call teenagers, or adolescents, covers that period midway between springtime and summer. As what happens to the trees and the blossoms during March determines the fruit, so the experiences of teenagers help mould their maturity. Some youths, like some fruits, ripen too soon, and others never seem to ripen at all, but there are others who fulfill the best aspirations of an older generation.

The psychology of teenagers is as important as it is interesting. The three dominant characteristics are: interiority, imitation and restlessness.

Interiority: A trait often missed because of the energy of youth is its consciousness of solitude and its sense of aloofness born of the realization that a kind of barrier is thrown up between itself and the world. Boys try sometimes to overcome this barrier by shaving before their time, thus leaping the wall between adolescence and manhood; girls affect it in dress or other mannerisms in order to bridge the gap. Gestures are clumsy, uneasy, ungraceful; arms seem too long and always in the way; words have little value for exchange purposes with adults in establishing contact with the grown-up world. There are more images than ideas in the interior world, which may account in part for the inability to establish rapport with others. Sometimes this very ineptitude increases interiority and drives the youth back into himself or herself. Because exterior actions do not always give release to the inner world, the teenager often has recourse to an inner world of images where he or she has an interior adventure, picturing himself as a hero on a football field, or herself as married to a prince. Movies are popular because they are a good feeder for such daydreams and hopes. The general picture, however, is of one who has suddenly arrived at a growing interior depth but, not knowing its value, expresses himself or herself badly.

Imitation: There is a profound philosophical reason for imitation. The ego is under the imperative and need of emerging from itself as a chrysalis; the interior is bursting to affirm its personality. Imitation becomes a substitute for originality. Originality commits the youth to effort, labor, pain, perseverance and sometimes the scorn of others; but imitation gives one the needed exteriorization through a kind of social conformism. Locked up in itself, youth must emerge. Since it is harder to be oneself, and at that age one does not quite know what is oneself, it becomes a hero-worshipper; hence the fan clubs, fanaticism for players of percussion instruments, the idolizing of some so-called movie star.

That is why in the high-school age one finds very few who ever dress outside of the pattern set by a few. The creative minority in adult life is few; therefore the youth must not be taken to task for imitation. This mimicry could be dangerous if what was idolized were low; but it can be also one of the ennobling influences of youth if those who are imitated are noble, good and patriotic. Youth imitates because it wants to create and creation marks the end of interiority in a constructive way.

Restlessness: Perhaps a better description of restlessness would be a mercurial affection. There is extreme mobility in youth, due to the multitude of impressions which flood the soul. Life is multiple; there is little harmony because of the great variety of appeals from the external world. Hence the appeal of certain youths for a certain type of loud music; it provides a muscular outlet for sense energy which has not yet been rationalized. Because of this agitation, it is difficult for a youth to fix his or her attention on any one object; perseverance in study is hard; the impulsions of the moment solicit with a loud voice. This could end in delinquency if the activity never found a target. But at the same time, like the other characteristics, it can also be the salvation of the youth, for he is really running around the circumference of human experience in order to decide on which particular segment he will settle for life. He tours the world of professions, avocations and positions and then decides in which he will repose. Once this energy becomes canalized, focused and rationalized, it becomes the beginning of a life's work and an adolescent begins to be what God intended him to be — a man who in loving virtue knows how to love a woman, a friend and his country.

23

THE LOVES OF YOUTH

EVERY YOUTH IS FULL OF incertitude and a latent anxiety. This is because life has not yet been brought to unity. What is immediate and present solicits him with such force that there is little thought of overall goal and purpose. To cover up this uneasiness, a youth often imagines what a psychologist might call a Super-self. It is not another image of himself, but rather the image of something that will complete himself and bring him to unity. This Super-self is what we desire to be to complete our personality and what we sometimes fear we never will be. It is almost like the acorn imagining the oak, the bud imagining the flower, and the foundation the roof. It is the completion of all aspirations, the realization of our dreams. "Young men dream dreams; old men see visions" (cf. Joel 3:1). The young look ahead, the aged look back. The young, like the rivulet, look forward to the sea which will immerse them in joy; the old, like the sea, look backwards to the rivulets.

Hence in the love of youths there is a tendency

to admire those who complete its incompleteness. Basically, this is nothing else than a love of God Who alone can satisfy all the aspirations of the heart. He, therefore, who believes himself completely satisfied, who never reaches out for a perfection which he has not at this moment, is incapable of loving. Every youth falls in love with the image of the possible, that is, with his dream walking, his emptiness filled, and his yearnings realized. Gustave Thibon once said that "every woman promises that which only God can give." By this he meant that the love every heart wants is the infinite; woman seems to give this to man, but actually what man wants is not the lovable but Love which is Divine. In literature, it is not uncommon to find women described as the image of the possible; for example, Beatrice for Dante. No one really knows if Beatrice ever existed. But certainly her influence was greater because she remained as the possible ideal. Everyone carries within himself a blueprint of his ideal. Some day this ideal is seen and, though it is called "love at first sight," it could conceivably be that which was always loved, but never seen before. Our ideal, or Super-self may even induce us to put ourselves in situations favorable to seeing it realized, as a man who loves dueling seeks out the company of those who duel. Youth seeks out the person who will complete the interior circuit, who will fulfill a desire which is basically for God, but which for a time substitutes for Him. Everyone loves the whole more than the part. Therefore everyone loves God more than His lover reflected in creatures. In most, however, this love is unconscious rather than conscious.

The great mystery of life is really not that we want to be loved, but that we are loved. We need love because we are imperfect; but why anyone should love the imperfect is not easy to understand. That is why all lovers consider themselves unworthy. The beloved is on a pedestal, the lover is on his knees professing his unworthiness. Love always comes as an undeserved gift. To abandon or be unfaithful to that love is to hurt the whole personality, for it destroys the image that was first there. The destruction of the image of the possible is to condemn oneself to a heartache as one feels the truth of the cruel words of Ovid: "I cannot live either with you or without you."

This Super-self, or ideal, or image of the possible manifests itself in different ways in a young man and a young woman. In the former, there is a delight found in giving reasons why she is the ideal. Thus does he rationalize his ideal, proving to himself and to others that the ideal has come to life. In the latter, however, she strives to intensify the idea that she is the ideal by seeming flight. To attract she appears to fly, thus making her more of an ideal to the pursuer. But in each case the true and absolute ideal is not found. That is God. But it is only later on in life that youth realizes that what he wanted was "the love we fall just short of in all love" — the love of the Infinite with "passionless passion and wild tranquility!"

INNER PEACE

24

"Getting Away With It"

BEHIND EVERY ATTEMPT TO "get away with it" is the belief that one will never be found out. If there is only one check on the books, one can be reasonably secure that there will be no discovery of the theft, but if there is a second check by a master bookkeeper, one is less inclined to commit the crime. Nothing so much conduces to evil as the belief that this world is all, and that beyond there is not a further judgment on the way we have lived and thought. If this world is all, then why not get all you can out of it and at any cost, providing you can "get away with it"?

Contrary to this philosophy is that of Our Lord Who said: "Nothing is concealed that will not be revealed, nor hidden that will not be made known" (Lk 12:2). Everything tends to emerge from the darkness into the light where it may stand in its true judgment. Seeds that are buried seek to pierce their grave; trees in a thick forest bend in order to more readily absorb the light; shells deep in the sea grope their way to the shore. So the lives of men, however deeply they bury their crimes, will one day push themselves to the Light of Judgment where "each man will be judged according to his works."

Modern psychology is based on the assumption that even in this world man really "gets away" with nothing. His secret hates, his hidden sins, his flippant treading upon the laws of morality — all of these leave their traces in his mind, his heart and his unconsciousness. Like the boy in the ancient fable who concealed in his blouse a fox which he had stolen. While denying his guilt, the fox ate away his entrails. The thousands of people stretched out on psychoanalytical couches may deny morality and guilt, but even while making their denial a real psychologist can see their mind being eaten away. There is nothing hidden that will not be revealed.

Inside of every heart are passions and wishes, hopes and fears, hatreds and lusts, evil intents and hidden guilts; one day all of these shadowy dwellers of the mental underworld will work their way up either to a confession of guilt or else to mental and physical signs of the denial of that guilt. Anyone is free to deny morality, but he is not free to escape the effects of its violation. Sin is written on faces, in the brain. It is seen in the shifting eyes and the hidden fears of night.

If a man knows that his thefts will one day be discovered, he will take every possible means to make recompense before discovery. If a man knows that one day everything he did will not only be revealed to God but also to his fellowmen, he will purge himself of them, that what was before a debit may now be a credit. To such a soul there is nothing more foolish than trying to "get away with it."

Psychiatry is not as much a modern discovery as it is a modern need. Its method has been known for centuries, but there was never the occasion to apply it, because in other ages men knew they could not "get away with it." Their purgations, reparations and amendments were settled on their knees in prayer, rather than on their back on a couch. But at that moment when the Divine and morality were denied, society came face to face with handling the mental effects which that very denial entailed. The crimes were not new, for people could snap their fingers just as much against the moral law in the days of faith as now. In those days when they did wrong, they knew it was wrong. They lost the road, but they never threw away the map. But today when men do wrong they call it right. This creates in addition to the moral problem which is denied, a *mental* problem. And that is where much psychiatry comes in. There is nothing new about the discovery that the reality we refuse to face we bury in our unconscious mind. What is new is the need to treat those who break the law and deny the law; who live by freedom and refuse to accept its consequences. Every soul that violates a law of God sooner or later turns states-evidence against himself. The long tongue of wrong-doing will not be quiet. Deny though he may the Divine Judge, his anxieties and fears reveal that there is already a judge seated in his own conscience, condemning even when society approves, and re-proving when he himself would deny. There is no secrecy for wickedness. The fear of God may have vanished from modern civilization, but the fear of man has taken its place and therefore made us unhappy. To fear God is to dread hurting one we love, like a child before a devoted father. To fear man is to shrink from threats and cruelty. One day a Great Book will be opened and there even every idle word we uttered will be recorded. Whatever is spoken in darkness will be brought to light, for in the final analysis no man "gets away" with anything.

25

Self-discipline

The philosophy of self-expression is so much taken for granted today that few there are who analyze its meaning. Self-expression is right when it means acting according to reason and our higher nature; it is wrong when it means acting in accordance with our instincts and lower nature. A hunter is self-expressive in the right way when he hunts animals in season; he is wrong when he goes hunting mothers-in-law, in season or out of season. Those who identify self-expression with license, or the right to do whatever they please, think that self-discipline is self-destruction, but actually it is only taming the lower for the sake of the higher. The violinist does not break the string when he tunes it to concert-pitch; the sculptor does not destroy the marble when he chisels it to produce the image.

When the chastening of self comes from the outside, it is affiliation; when it comes from the inside by an act of our own will, it is self-discipline. In either case, its purpose is the emergence of a truer and better character. God never permits an affliction except for the purposes of purification. Scripture goes so far as to say that "whomever the Lord loves tenderly He chastens and rebukes" (Rv 3:19). A young man who loves a young woman wants to see her dressed in a most becoming manner; she, too, suits the color of her dress and the fashion of her hair to his taste. All egotistic wishes are expunged for the sake of the beloved. God, too, sometimes shakes all the leaves off the trees which surround our self-existence in order that we may see the heavens.

Sometimes even the death of a child is God's way of making parents look beyond this world to the next. When a shepherd finds that his sheep have exhausted the lower pastures, but refuse to climb to greener pastures, he will take a young lamb in his arms to the heights of the mountain side, and the other sheep will follow. The mother eagle gets her young to fly by pecking away pieces of the nest bit by bit, until finally the young have to leave their temporary security. God, too, sometimes has to disturb man in his economic security, lest he think that it is the only security there is.

But over and above this passive discipline from without, there is an active discipline. There is no evil propensity of the heart that is so powerful that it cannot be subdued by discipline. Every man is like an onion. His superficial self has many layers of skins, and at the center of them all is his real self. Self-abnegation tears off all the outer deceptions and finally reveals our true character. One of the reasons why so few know God is because they do not know themselves. They live in a world of make-believe where nothing is real, and thus miss the Ground of all Reality.

We of the Western World have begun to falsely believe that a character is made by external works, and that it matters little what a man does or thinks or wills on the inside. But this can be an escape, for a man can plunge into work to try to forget himself, just as a man can plunge into alcohol to forget himself. When anything goes wrong, the undisciplined blames things — as the golfer blames the clubs for the poor shot, or the clumsy carpenter the tools for inferior work. Actually the fault lies within the disordered and selfish self.

If a man gives up his wealth, his time, and his energy to others, but actually does not give up himself, he has given up nothing. But he who has had some wealth and some honor, but has denied himself, then he is most free. When Our Blessed Lord said that a man must hate himself, He did not mean those qualities in him which make for God-likeness, but rather those barnacles of selfishness which prevent him from becoming all that Love has destined for him. There has been no greater secret of inner peace ever given than in the words of John the Baptist when he saw Our Lord coming: "He must increase; I must decrease" (Jn 3:30).

26

KINDNESS

MANY PEOPLE WHO ARE very kind in their own homes and offices can become very unkind and selfish once they get behind the steering wheel of an automobile. This is probably due to the fact that in their own home they are known; in the automobile they have the advantage of anonymity and hence can be almost brutal without the fear of discovery. To be kind out of fear of others thinking we are unkind is not real kindness, but rather a disguised form of egotism.

The word "kindness" is derived from kindred or kin, and therefore implies an affection which we bear naturally to those who are our flesh and blood. The original and archetypal kindness is that of a parent for a child and a child for a parent, an idea which is preserved in the German language where *Kind* means child. Gradually the word gained in extension until it embraced everyone whom we are to treat as a relative. Unkindness is therefore unnaturalness.

Because kindness is related to love, it follows

that the kind person loves another not for the pleasure the other person gives, nor because the other person can do us a kindness in return, but because the other person is lovable in himself. The basic reason why everyone is lovable is because God made him.

Since God finds us lovable because He put some of His love into us, so we can find others lovable because we put some of our love into them. But to do this implies a basic kindness which is always prepared to be pleasant with other people. If we start with the belief that most people in the world are crooks, it is amazing how many crooks we find. If, however, we go into the world with the assumption that every one is nice, we are constantly running into nice people. To a great extent the world is what we make it. We get back what we give. If we sow hate, we reap hate; if we scatter love and gentleness we harvest love and happiness. Other people are like a mirror which reflects back on us the kind of image we cast. The kind man bears with the infirmities of others, never magnifies trifles and avoids a spirit of fault finding. He knows that the trouble with most people in the world is that they are unloved. No one cares for them either because they are ugly or nasty, or troublesome, or so-called bores. To a great extent their character is made by the resentment they feel toward others who are unkind. One of life's greatest joys comes from loving those whom no one else loves. Thus do we imitate Our Heavenly Father Who certainly cannot see much in any of us creatures that is very attractive. It is curious that most people are more kind to the blind than they are to the deaf. Aristotle commented upon this fact, saying that sight is the most spiritual of all the senses and hearing the most material. For that reason we are moved by sympathy towards those who are afflicted in the most spiritual way. This psychological explanation, however, in no way justifies a want of kindness to either.

Kindness towards the afflicted becomes compassion, which means a suffering with, or an entering into the distress and the pains of others as if they were our own. It enlarges the interest of the heart beyond all personal interest and prompts us to give either what we have in the form of alms, or the giving of one's talent as a doctor may treat a poor patient, or the giving of one's time which is sometimes the hardest thing of all to give. The truly compassionate and kind man who gives up his time for others manages to find time. Like the bread, miraculously multiplied, he gives, and yet he gathers up for himself more than he gave.

Many psychiatrists today know very well that all they have to do to help certain distressed minds is to listen to their stories. Convince the anxious heart that you know the secret of his anxiety and he is already half cured. Even if we can convince the enemy that we have no bitterness in our heart against him, his arm will fall helpless at his side. All mental abnormalities have their roots in selfishness, all happiness has its roots in kindness. But to be really kind, one must see in everyone an immortal soul to be loved for God's sake. Then everyone is precious.

27

FEAR AND ETHICS

MOST NEUROSES ARE BULWARKS against fear. Many psychologists and physicians have come to adopt this thesis inasmuch as fear does provoke some kind of self-defense. It is actually not fear that is feared; the enemy is the tension between the conscience and what has happened. Fear is like the gauge on a steam boiler. It merely registers pressure.

The simplest way but the worst way to remove fear from the conscious mind is to repress it — that is, to relegate it into unconsciousness. When unexpected visitors come to the house, a housewife will take old linen and dirty shirts which lie about the front room and toss them into the cellar. The mind does the same thing; it defends itself against tormenting sensations by throwing them into the unconsciousness.

The effects of suppressing fear are manifold. First, on the physical side, they may be palpitation, migraine, cramps, convulsions, etc. On the mental side, the repressed fear comes out as anger, depression and surliness. One psychologist tells the story of a small boy who wept copiously whenever he heard bells tolled for a funeral. He had often wished that his parents were dead, but he repressed the wish. He was afraid as a result of the wish and he escaped it by weeping. His fear resulted from the guilt of wishing his parents dead and he sublimated it by tears.

Lady Macbeth had induced her ambitious husband to murder the King, their guest, while he slept, and then to assume the crown. When her husband is shaken by the act she reminds him:

> *"These deeds must not be thought*
> *After these ways, so it will make us mad."*

This is an excellent description of the pathological effects of the murderer's endeavor to escape fear. She is trying to drown conscience by saying that one must not think of the deed in terms of right and wrong. Yet all the while that she is repressing it she is inducing her own madness. She tells her husband to wash his hands and then to smear the grooms with blood. Since he is afraid to do so, she kills the grooms herself and then smears their bodies with the blood. Then she exclaims:

> *"My hands are your color but I shame*
> *To wear a heart so white….*
> *A little water clears us of this deed."*

Here she tries to convince herself and her husband again that one must not seek to have a clean heart; that there is no judge within the human breast, and that all one has to do is to clear oneself of the external consequences.

Conscience still produces its effects; she who tried to deny it now has a compulsion neurosis which expresses itself in the constant washing of hands:

> *"Who would have thought the old man*
> *To have so much blood in him....*
> *Will these hands ne'er be clean?"*

First she thought that the guilt of the murder could be cleansed by washing away the blood; now she has to wash away the fear of guilt, as she admits with her husband that all the waters of the seven seas are not enough to wash the blood from her hands.

There are some people who wash their hands after touching door knobs and who repeat this process as much at ten times before they get out of the house. This signifies a need of cleansing and it is thought that the external washings will be a substitute for the moral and inner washing which is denied because of repressed guilt. This does not mean to say that all those who suffer from guilt have violated some moral principle; but it does mean that those who have done so can never expect to have their fears lifted by mere treatment of the external symptoms.

Medical treatment in dealing with fear should never neglect the moral principles which may possibly be behind fear and their manifestations in body and mind. Even Freud has admitted that from a medical point of view the unscrupulous method of satisfying every instinct may make the patient worse. Ethics is the very essence of sound medical treatment.

28

REST AND MEDITATION

MODERN MAN WOULD BE FAR happier if he would take a little time off to meditate. As the Old Testament prophet said: "'Peace, peace,' they say, though there is no peace. They are odious; they have done abominable things, yet they are not at all ashamed, they know not how to blush" (Jr 6:14-15). The Gospel tells us that Our Blessed Lord withdrew Himself from the crowds into the wilderness and prayed. Martha, who was too busy about many things, was told that only one thing was necessary. A life of faith with peace of soul can be cultivated only by periodical isolation from the cares of the world.

There are various kinds of weariness: weariness of the body, which can be satisfied under any tree or even on a pillow of stone; weariness of the brain, which needs the incubation of rest for new thought to be born; but hardest of all to satisfy is weariness of heart, which can be healed only by communion with God.

Silence helps speech; retirement helps thinking. A contemporary of Abraham Lincoln tells us that he spent three weeks with Lincoln just after the Battle of Bull Run: "I could not sleep. I was repeating the part that I was to play in a public performance. The hour was past midnight. Indeed, it was coming near to dawn, when I heard low tones coming from the room where the President slept. The door was partly open. I instinctively walked in and there I saw a sight which I shall never forget. It was the President, kneeling beside an open Bible. The light was turned low in the room. His back was turned toward me. For a moment I was silent, as I stood looking in amazement and wonder. Then he cried out in tones so pleading and sorrowful: 'O God who heard Solomon in the night that he prayed for wisdom, hear me; I cannot lead this people, I cannot guide the affairs of this nation without Your help. I am poor and weak and sinful. O God, who heard Solomon when he cried to You, hear me and save this nation'."

One wonders how many of our public officials in the great burdens that are laid upon them ever cry to God for help. When the United Nations held its first meeting in San Francisco, fearful that we might offend the atheists, it was decided to keep a minute of silence instead of praying fearlessly to God to illumine and guide the nations. It was in the moment of Peter's failure in fishing that Our Lord said: "Launch out into the deep" (Lk 5:4). It is in the times of our failures that the soul must draw away from the shores.

What the Savior promises in the retirement is "rest for your souls." Rest is a gift; it is not earned; it is not the payment for finishing a job; it is the dowry of grace. Greed, envy, wealth and avarice think of rest in terms of the good things of the world; true rest is the stilling of passions, the control of wavering ambitions, the joy of a quiet conscience. There is no rest until life has been made intelligible. Most of the restlessness of souls today comes from not knowing why they are here, or where they are going, and they refuse to take time out to solve that problem. Until it is solved, nothing is solved. There is not even much sense in going on living unless one knows why he is living.

Driving power is always associated with inner repose; otherwise energy is explosiveness and imprudent action. They that *wait* upon the Lord shall *renew* their strength. The renewal of strength is less physical than it is spiritual. A tired soul makes a tired body more often than a tired body makes a tired soul. The rest which Christianity enjoins is less cessation from work than it is freedom from the anxieties that come from guilt and avarice. Spiritual refreshment in prayer, retreat, and meditation are the most potent influences for restoring harmony to the thousands of nervous patients. Life, like music, must have its rhythm of silence as well as sound.

The rest which retirement and contemplation give is not just a rest from toil, but it is even a rest in toil. The peace of Christ is not a hot-house plant; it raises its head for the storms; it is peace for the battle and joy of conscience for those who assail conscience. The world cannot give it; the world cannot take it away. It is not given by outward circumstance; it rules in the heart; it is an inward state. To be spiritually minded is to have rest.

GIVING

29

Better to Give than Receive

The vast majority of the people in Western civilization are engaged in the task of getting. Strange as it may seem, the Christian ethic is founded on the opposite principle, that it is more blessed to *give* than to receive. Both the opportunity and the burden of fulfilling this Divine mandate fall principally upon those of us who live in a civilization that has been abundantly blessed by God. Did you know that the per capita income of the United States is over $22,000 a year (1992 figures) and that we pay more in *taxes* than most people in the world earn to keep body and soul together?

We are, of course, a nation helping the socially disinherited people of the world; we have even given an example of loving our enemies in war by helping their economic restoration. But here our concern is less with the national spirit of giving, than it is with the personal spirit. The reason it is more blessed to give than to receive is because it helps to detach the soul from the material and the temporal in order to ally it with a spirit of altruism and charity which is the essence of religion. Cicero once said that "men resemble gods in nothing so much as in doing good to their fellow creatures." Aristotle says that by narrowness and selfishness, by envy and ill will, men degenerate into beasts and become wolves and tigers to one another; but by goodness and love, by mutual compassion and helpfulness, men become gods to one another.

The history of the Jews reveals how much their temporal blessing was consecrated to the service of God and to aiding the poor. In the best days of their history, their tithes and offerings, their thank-offerings and their free-will offerings, were on a scale of splendid munificence; nor did they lose thereby for they were constantly thanking God for their many blessings. Even today that same spirit of generosity has characterized these people, not only to their own brethren, but also to Protestants and Catholics as well.

On a smaller scale, it will be found that the unity of a community depends to a great extent upon the services and kindnesses of one individual to another. The farming population of any country in the world is a perfect example of this altruism. At harvest time, each farmer helps every other farmer, and when there is a death in the family, willing hands are always found to pick the corn and cut the wheat.

There is not always the same spirit in the large

cities, partly due to the anonymity of the masses, and partly due to competition. Where most people we meet are strangers, there is a tendency to lock one's self in his shell. One notices this particularly in driving an automobile. Men who are very gentle at home and kind to friends, become like raging beasts growling at the stupidity of every other driver once they get behind a wheel where anonymity protects them.

Giving is really a divinely appointed way of acknowledging the mercies of God. We have indeed nothing to offer anyway that we have not received, and yet He is pleased to accept our offerings as tokens of our gratitude. Egotism makes the self the center; altruism and charity make the neighbor the center. Only on the principle of giving can the inequalities of the human race be adjusted, can the strong help the weak, and social peace reign among men. Many a man when he was poor had a heart that was open to every call of pity, but as riches increased he set his heart more upon them. The massing of wealth has a peculiar effect on the soul; it intensifies the desire of getting. What is often lust in youth is avarice in old age. Could they but expose themselves to the great joy of giving and respond to pity's claim, they would sense the great thrill in benevolence. Great as the pleasure is in receiving, greater is the pleasure in benevolence.

There is an old story about a Scotsman, Lord

Braco, who was very rich and miserly and who had great stores of gold and silver in his vaults. One day a farmer said to him: "I will give you a shilling if you will but let me see all your gold and silver." Braco consented. The farmer gave him the shilling saying: "Now I am as rich as you are. I have looked at your gold and silver, and that is all you can do with it."

There is more happiness in rejoicing in the good of others, than in rejoicing in our own good. The receiver rejoices in his good; the giver in the joy of others and to such comes the peace nothing in the world can give.

30

THE SPIRIT OF SERVICE

THE DESIRE FOR DISTINCTION is one of the most radical principles of our nature; even though it be crucified and buried, in an unexpected moment it revives and rises again in power. The subtle passion is strongest in the middle period of life. It comes in between the love of pleasure which besets youth and the love of gain which besets old age. Opposed to all egotism and selfishness is the ideal of usefulness and service. He only is great of heart who floods the world with great affection; he only is great of mind who stirs the world with pure thoughts. Our Divine Lord gave the key to greatness when He said that He came not to be ministered to, but to minister to others. Such service of others as He inspired must be loving in the sense that out of no fountain save that of love can such amazing and endless acts of helpfulness flow.

Loving and serving are inseparable. Such service, too, is self-denying and ego-effacing. To continue helping day after day in the midst of reproach and opposition and rejection means that one is governed by a higher law than the desire of applause. Such service cannot be bought, for no gold could purchase it, neither does it need to be bought, for it is freely rendered.

Unless a man sets out to help his neighbor in the spirit of love he will never overcome those faulty tendencies in his nature which constantly try to drag it down. Some 2,500 years ago Aristotle remarked that all of our degrading tendencies arranged themselves under two heads of temper and desire — bad temper and ill-regulated desire. When one is not present the other is, and sometimes one and sometimes the other appear at different periods in the life of the same man. Inasmuch as service is a voluntary undertaking of a work in obedience to the Higher Will, it is a corrective of these tendencies.

It is corrective first of all of temper in its everyday form of self-assertion and pride. The man who serves from his heart cannot indulge in egotism. He represses self in order to make his service the more kindly. Each five minutes of conscientious service has the effect of keeping the ego disciplined and of bidding it submit to a Higher and more Righteous Will. Self-asserting man always tries to make an inferior feel the full weight of his petty importance and thus, sooner or later, self-assertion becomes tyranny. Helpfulness, on the other hand, makes the ego appear inferior in order that the neighbor may be exalted.

Irregulated desire is also crushed by affection-
ate helpfulness. Desire is irregulated when it makes
self the center of all things and even the law to which
all others must submit. This evil can be cured
radically only by making God the object of desire.
One then sacrifices many of his luxuries and pleasures in order to assist the needy and the less
fortunate. In doing this, character is incidentally
improved inasmuch as it detracts one from sensuous
and indulgent ease which leads to the spoiling of
character.

Even upon material works God has stamped
the law of sympathetic service. It is written out in the
clouds of the sky to seek to die in the service of rain.
The little streams flee decaying self-content by emp-
tying themselves into the vastness of the ocean. The
mountains too are in service. They are like giant
hands raised to catch and redistribute the moisture,
sending it down across the plains in healthful and
life-giving streams. Not a drop of water leads a
selfish life; not a wind blast is without its mission.
What God has imposed upon nature by law He
intended we should impose upon ourselves in virtue
of our free will. The waters and the clouds and the
mountains and even the earth itself which spends
itself in giving life to the seed — all of these rebuke
the man who refuses to live for his fellowman. In
doing good, everything in God's universe gets good.
Service of others is the highest service of self, and the

best way for any man to grow in grace is to move forward in helpfulness. The mill wheel will cease to revolve when the waters of the rushing stream are cut off; the moving train stops when the glowing heat cools within the hidden chamber; and charity in this world will degenerate into mere professional schedules and statistical averages without inspiration, without power and without love as men forget the inspiration of Him Who said: "No one has greater love than this, to lay down one's life for one's friends" (Jn 15:13).

31

How to Give

"MAKE FRIENDS FOR YOURSELVES with the mammon of iniquity" (Lk 16:9) is one of the mysterious sayings of Our Blessed Lord to those who do not understand its meaning. "Mammon" is a Syrian word meaning money, and Jesus calls it the "mammon of iniquity" because those to whom Our Lord spoke too often used it for unjust and iniquitous purposes. A dollar bill in our pocket, if it could speak, might scandalize us in telling us the things for which it was spent, the transactions in which it had taken part, and the sinful pleasures it had bought. Our Lord tells us that there is a time when it fails, for the man who has money is only a steward. Death says to every man: "Give an account of your stewardship for you can be steward no longer" (Lk 16:2). Money simply cannot be transferred to the world beyond.

Here we come to the purpose of money according to the Savior. Give away money to those who are in need, for by relieving their necessity you will make friends of those who will intercede for the salvation of your soul. Money will not buy heaven; but it will make friends for us that will help us when we fail. "Inasmuch as you did it for the least of these My brethren, you did it for Me" (Mt 25:40). Those who have been helped by our charity will lead us before the throne saying: "This is he of whom we have spoken and who did so much for us in the life below."

A traveler in a foreign country exchanges his own currency for that of the other land. So too the wealth we have here can be exchanged for spiritual wealth in the next world where "neither moth nor rust destroy, and where thieves neither break in nor steal" (Mt 6:20).

What is the psychology of those who will never touch their capital for charity? They keep piling up more and more reserves, each new addition becoming as sacred as the one before. The answer is that every man is made for the infinite, which is God. But his reason becomes blinded through prejudice or sin, so he substitutes another infinite which is money. He then wants more and more of *having*, instead of more and more of *being* which is life in God. No matter how many hairs a man has in his head, it hurts to have even one pulled out. No matter how much capital a man has, it hurts to touch even a cent of it. He knows "he can't take it with him" so he denies there is any place to go.

The Christian way is to use money that those

who are helped may be our intercessors in heaven. A wealthy man once told his maid to give away to his neighbors the fruits from his garden in order that she might make friends of them. Wealth thus becomes worthy of its name, which is weal.

A wealthy woman once got into heaven where St. Peter pointed out the mansion of her chauffeur. She said: "If that is my chauffeur's home, think what mine will be." St. Peter pointed out to her one of the more humble bungalows of heaven saying: "That's your home." "Oh," she said, "I could never live there." St. Peter answered: "Sorry, Madam, but that is the best I could do with the materials you sent me."

There is much money given away, but little of it is used for the soul. Some give it away in order to have their name glorified on the door of a hospital or a university. Men who have had very little education are conspicuous for endowing libraries that they might create the impression of being learned, which they are not. Our Lord said: "Let not your left hand know what your right hand gives" (cf. Mt 6:3). This was followed by the second principle of giving: The gift must be offered for a Divine reason. The cup of cold water will be given a reward a hundredfold if it is given in Christ's name.

Some years ago the cloister of Carmelite nuns was opened to the public on the feast of St. Thérèse. Many curious people poured in to see those women who led a life of silence, prayer and penance. One man who could not understand their life called the attention of a young and beautiful nun to the finest residence in the city which stood on the opposite hill. He said to her: "Sister, if you could have had that home, with all the wealth, luxury and pleasure that went with it, would you have left it to enter the Carmelites?" She answered: "Sir, that was my home."

There is so much giving that is wasted because it is not done for the soul. The world thinks that the highest things must be used for the lowest, for example, the intellect to make surplus wealth. The man of God believes that the lowest must be used for the highest, that is, money must be spent to help spread Divine Truth, to solace the afflicted and to cure the sick that their souls may be free to work out their salvation. The truest answer to "You can't take it with you" is: "You can, provided you give it away." Then it is stored up as merit in the next life.

MAN

32

PROGRESS

G K. CHESTERTON ONCE SAID: "There is one thing in the world that never makes any progress and that is the idea of progress." By this he meant that unless we have a fixed concept of what progress really means we can never know that we are making any headway. Unfortunately, there are many who, instead of working toward an ideal, change it, and call it progress. One would never know he was making progress from Chicago to San Francisco if San Francisco became identified with New York. Only when the goal is fixed and definite do we ever have a target and the energy to shoot the arrow.

Everything in earth's geology and everything on the earth's surface point to a future: the impulse of a river is forward into the sea; the little child tells what he intends to be when he is a man; thoughts fly on wings toward tomorrow; all these impulses which carry us onward imply a future under God. Those who lose sight of the goal often concentrate on mere motion and try to derive pleasure from it. They delight in turning the pages of a book, but never finish the story; they pick up brushes, but never finish a picture; they travel the seas, but know no ports. Their zest is not in the achievement of a destiny but rather in gyration and action for the mere sake of movement.

Perfection is being, not doing; it is not to affect an act but to achieve a character. There is nothing that makes life unhappier than its meaninglessness, and life is devoid of meaning only when it is without purpose. There are tens of thousands of minor purposes, but the one great purpose is the perfection of our character from a moral point of view. Infinite as are the varieties of life, he who has not found out directly how to make everything converge to the sanctification of his own soul has missed the meaning of life.

The son of Confucius once said to him: "I apply myself with diligence to every kind of study, and neglect nothing that could render me clever and ingenious, but still I do not advance." To which Confucius answered: "Omit some of your pursuits and you will get on better." The life of a man is vagrant, changeful, desultory, like that of children chasing butterflies, until he has discovered for himself why he is here and where he is going. Rivers do not grow shallower as they roll away from their sources, and the heart's river need not be any exception. It should flow on, widening and deepening until it meets the great ocean of Divine Love for which it is destined, and mingles with it.

Dissatisfaction sometimes can be the motive of true progress. Dissatisfied with the pen, man invented the printing press; dissatisfied with the chariot and the locomotive, he invented the airplane. There is implanted in everyone an impulse which drives the spirit to beat its wings like an imprisoned eagle in the cages of this earth until there is blood on its plumes. Did hearts but analyze this urge that is within them, which drives them away from the actual to the possible and makes them dig in the desert of their lives for new living springs, and climb every mountain to get a better look at heaven, they would see that they are being drawn back again to God, from Whom they came.

To stay complacently where we are in our spiritual life is to be as a tree that might congratulate itself that it is higher than the shrubs, or to be like a caterpillar that should stay exultant with its spots and stripes whilst the glorious life of the butterfly is untasted. No man is living who is resting on his own laurels, as no one is happy who says that he lives on his memories. Past laurels must be put aside as man must press forward to that supernal vocation to which he is called, forgetting the things that are behind. The bird must forget its nest, the seed its husk, the flower its bud, and unless these are forgotten we can never reach the goal. Both brooding and boasting are alike to be discouraged, for the happiness of life is in the prospect of the best and the holiest.

33

THE MASS-MAN

A NEW TYPE OF MAN IS multiplying in the modern world, and if there be any reader who recognizes his own portrait herein, let him take pause, reflect, and change. The new man is the mass-man, who no longer prizes his individual personality, but who seeks to be submerged in the collectivity or crowd.

This mass-man may be recognized by the following traits:

1. He is without originality of judgment; does no other reading except what is found in a daily newspaper, or picture magazine, or an occasional novel. He has only a different point of view to give on a common subject, but no new principle or solution.

2. He hates tranquility, meditation, silence or anything which gives him leisure to penetrate into the depths of his soul. He needs noise, crowds, the radio or TV, whether he listens to the latter or not.

3. Evasion or escape from self is a necessity. Alcohol, cocktails, detective stories, or movies are

taken in steady doses to fill up the emptiness of the hour. As the genius loves concentration, he seeks dispersion, particularly sex, in order that the excitement of the moment may dispel consideration of the problem of life.

4. He seeks to be influenced rather than to influence, is sensitive to propaganda, to the excitations of publicity and generally has one favorite columnist who does his thinking for him.

5. He believes that every instinct should be satisfied, regardless of whether or not its exercise is in accordance with right reason; he cannot understand self-denial, or self-discipline; he regards self-expression as identical with freedom, and at no vital points is he master of himself.

6. His beliefs of right and wrong change like the weathercock; he maintains positions which are nothing but a succession of contradictions, lays down mental tracks one month and the next month pulls them up. He is going nowhere, but he is sure he is on the way. He has no sense of gratitude toward the past and no sense of responsibility to the future. Nothing matters but distractions, so that life becomes cut up into a crazy pattern of successive instants none of which add up to make sense.

7. He identifies money and pleasure, and hence seeks to have much of the first in order to have much of the second. But the money must be obtained with as little effort as possible. The ego is the

center of everything and everything is to be related to it through the intermediary of money.

8. To break his solitude he has recourse to an ersatz communion with others, through night clubs, parties and collective distractions. But from each of these he returns more lonely than before, finally believing with Sartre that "hell is others."

9. Being a mass-man completely standardized, he hates superiority in others, either real or imagined. Scandals he loves because they seem to prove that others are no better than he. Religion he dislikes, the real reason being that by denying it he thinks he could then go on living as he does without remorse of conscience.

10. He might just as well go by a number as by a name he is so immersed in the crowd mind. Even the authority he invokes is anonymous. It is always "they." "They say," or "they are wearing," or "they are doing this." Anonymity becomes a protection against the assuming of responsibilities. In the big cities he feels freer because he is less known, but at the same time he hates it because it cancels his personal distinction. The perfect symbol of the impersonal mass-man is the social security number, which completes his alienation from himself.

These are the ten marks of the mass-man who is the raw material of every form of totalitarianism. Psychologically, he is also the unhappy man, full of despair, anxiety, fear, and afraid of the meaninglessness of life. But he is not hopeless if he would but enter into himself. The only reason he wants to be lost in the crowd is because he cannot bear his inner misery. It follows that he must detach himself from the masses and come to grips with himself. Flight is cowardice and escapism, especially flight into anonymity.

It takes a brave man to look into the mirror of his own soul to see written there the disfigurements caused by his own misbehavior. It is no truism to say men must be men, not atoms in a mass. Once man sees his self-inflicted wounds, the next step is to take them to the Divine Physician to be cured. It was to such tired mass-men that He made His appeal: "Come to Me all you who are weary and heavily burdened and… you will find rest for your souls" (Mt 11:28, 30).

34

A Recall to the Inner Life

A FATHER GAVE HIS LITTLE SON a cut-up puzzle of the world and asked him to put it together. The boy finished the picture in an amazingly short time. When the astonished father asked him how he did it, the boy answered: "There was a picture of a man on the other side; when I put the man together, the world came out all right." Such is the key to the understanding of all the political and economic problems of our day. Nothing ever happens to the world which does not first happen inside man. Wars are not made by politics, but by politicians with a certain philosophy of life. No explanation of war has ever been as clear as the biblical one which declares that wars are punishments on man for his sin. Not a punishment in the sense that God sends a war as a father spanks a child for an act of disobedience; but rather that a war follows a breakdown of morality, as thunder follows lightning, and as blindness follows the plucking out of the eye.

Those who are in middle age have lived through an era where war is more "normal" than peace. There has been literally fulfilled what Nietzsche proph-esied, namely, that the twentieth century would be a century of wars. War is a symptom of the break-down of civilization. There are only different de-grees of guilt among the combatants. All is not black on one side, and all is not white on another. When a body becomes diseased, the germ does not localize in one organ to the exclusion of all others; it infects the whole blood stream. So the evil of our day is the evil not of the East or the West, but of the world. It is of the world because men generally have become estranged from the true center of their spiritual life. Having ceased to fear God, in the sense of filial fear such as a child has for a father, they have begun to fear man with a servile fear, such as a slave has for a tyrant.

Modern man has become passive in the face of evil. He has so long preached a doctrine of false tolerance; has so long believed that right and wrong were only differences in a point of view, that now when evil works itself out in practice he is paralyzed to do anything against it. Political injustice, chica-nery in high office, and organized crime leave him cold. While keeping very busy and active on the outside, he is passive and inert on the inside, be-cause he rarely enters into his own heart. Remedying the evil therefore falls to agencies and mechanical realities external to man. No government or state can put the screws on personal freedom, unless the citizens have already abdicated in themselves the basis of that freedom, namely, their responsibility to God.

Having lost his inward unity, man is more and more compelled to seek the unity outside himself in the unity of organization. Disclaiming all responsibility, he surrenders it more and more to the State. The sheep that will not obey the shepherd must be retrieved by a dog barking at their heels. The citizen who will not obey the moral laws of God, must be organized by a dictator snapping at their souls. The weakening of the inner spiritual life is the basic cause of the disharmony and discord which prevail throughout the world. The forcible organization of the chaos created by the enfeeblement of the moral sense always calls forth some dictator who makes law personal rather than a reflection of the Eternal harmony that rules in the heavens.

A great burden is thrust upon men who call themselves religious. In this fatal hour, all of their energies should be spent recalling man to his spiritual destiny and summoning him to invoke the God Who made him. Instead of that there are some who would accuse their neighbors who also believe in God, of being disloyal to their country, or else of trying to impose their faith by force on their fellow citizens. Such lies do a disservice both to God and to country. And their supposed faith in God is to be questioned, because no one who loves God hates his neighbor, nor does he try to incite citizen against citizen through slander. Let those who call themselves Catholics, or Protestants, or Jews recall that the function of their religion is to intensify the spiritual life of man and not to empty the vials of bitterness into hearts, stirring up one against another. It is not to the politicians and the economists and the social reformers that we must look for the first steps in this spiritual recovery; it is to the professed religious. The nonreligious can help by repudiating those who come to them in the name of God or America and say that their neighbor does not love either. Religion must not be a cloak covering the dagger of hate!

35

Why We Are Not Better

THE REASON WHY WE ARE NOT better than we are is that we do not will to be better: the sinner and the saint are set apart only by a series of tiny decisions within our hearts. Opposites are never so close as in the realm of the spirit: an abyss divides the poor from the rich, and one may cross it only with the help of external circumstances and good fortune. The dividing line between ignorance and learning is also deep and wide: both leisure to study and a gifted mind would be required to turn an ignoramus into a learned man. But the passage from sin to virtue, from mediocrity to sanctity requires no "luck," no help from outer circumstances. It can be achieved by an efficacious act of our own wills in cooperation with God's grace.

St. Thomas tells us that, "We are not saints because we *will* not to be saints." He does not say, mind you, that we do not *want* to be saints: many of us do. But mere *wanting* is the wish that something shall come to pass without our acting to bring it about. *Willing* means that we plan to pay the necessary cost in effort and in sacrifice.

We often delude ourselves into imagining that we have willed to be better, when actually we have made many reservations, have determined there are many present practices we will not change; then the willing is merely an idle wish. The key to spiritual advancement is to be found in the Creed: "He descended into hell; the third day He arose again." Each of us, too, must make a descent into the subconsciousness, to the portions of our minds which we keep dark, for it is here that the unspoken reservations hide. These reservations are not easily seen by us, but they color everything that we do see; they act like so many colored windows, changing the truth of external reality as it reaches our conscious minds. Reality is distorted if we have such reservations as prejudice, habits of sin, pride, avarice and jealousy. Any of these can make honest judgment impossible for us. The truth is then twisted to fit our imperfections; we lie to ourselves in order not to have to change, not to abandon these prized habits of evil.

Most of us live out our lives with a false picture of ourselves which we will not surrender; we dread the pain of finding ourselves less noble than we like to believe. We strain reality through a sieve of self-love, keeping out whatever truth would hurt us. Using this private measurement of truth is as misguided as it would be to let our own preferences decide which key on the piano is middle C — and as useless. We might pretend that a key easier to reach was Middle C, and act accordingly; but we should make discords, instead of harmonies. Reality cannot be cowed to our wishes.

These reservations to which we cling — these attitudes we insist we will not surrender or change — affect our conscious judgments and make them untrue. Before we can ever emerge into the gladness of God's reality, we have to go down into the hell in which we hide these unadmitted faults. This requires us to make a thoroughgoing analysis of ourselves in the light of God's unchanging laws.

The "Don't kid yourself!" of slang is sound spiritual advice. Nothing so stands in the way of our progress towards God as egotism, and the egotist is always full of self-deceit, of "sacred" faults he will not renounce, nor even admit he has. That is why the egotist in all of us requires a pitiless searching-out of every hidden nook and corner of our minds. We need to see the self as it really is, and not as we pretend it is. We must love Truth more than we love self; we must be willing to surrender all our unguessed faults, if we are ever to be able to see the Truth as it is.

Nothing so cripples the spiritual life as these hidden "bugs" in the motor of our soul. They may be any one of several common faults such as self-seeking, bitterness towards others, jealousy and hate. Those who are trying to grow closer to God without self-analysis wonder why they suffer such frequent defeats: invariably it is because of the Trojan Horse within them, the unrecognized dominant fault. Until that is dug out and admitted before God, with a desire to destroy it, there will be no real spiritual progress. As St. Augustine has said, "He, Lord, is Your best servant who looks not so much to hear that from You which he himself wills, as rather to will that which he hears from You."

36

Revolution Starts with Man

There are any number of social and economic theories under discussion today, but all plans for changing the world boil down to two: we may reform institutions, or we may reform man.

Most of the "blueprint for perfection" writers begin with the assumption that all the ills of humanity can be charged against an institution, a thing: change that, they tell us, and all will be well. Some of their programs blame private property for our troubles, and would "reform" it into collective ownership. Others blame our parliamentary systems, and offer to "reform" them into dictatorships. Others blame the gold policy, and tell us to "reform" it into a silver policy. But in every instance the revolution is to be waged against something outside of man; the blame is placed, and the solution sought, in property, or government, or finance. Present-day reformers never blame man himself for the world's debacle, nor try to reform the individual.

This emphasis on institutions as the cure-all of the world has become so great that many reformers draw up a plan for peace and prosperity — and then demand that man himself shall change his nature to fit their plan. Human personality has become insignificant to them; the State is no longer seen as existing for man, but man is told he gains his meaning only in the service he can give the State. Man, under such a system, is dehumanized, depersonalized, poured into a dictatorial pattern, so that he will be molded into a mere servant of a nation, a race or a class.

This stubborn worship of a theory has had most appalling consequences in our day. To the theorist, it does not seem to matter that whole nations are deprived of liberty, that millions starve, that thousands are purged — so long as the theory is maintained in power. Instead of making the hat of governmental policy fit the head of man, the modern tendency is to cut off the head if it does not fit the hat — to demand that institutions, political schemes and social theories must prevail, no matter if their cost proves to be the destruction of man himself.

But there is a second method of reforming the world. This method is based on the belief that reform must begin with man. It holds that his nature must, indeed, adapt itself — but to a larger plan than any temporal theory, than any government or institution or blueprint for world order. This second method agrees that there must be a revolution, but not a revolution against something *outside* of man. It urges a revolt against the evil *within* man; his pride, his egotism, his selfishness, his envy and his avarice.

The second kind of revolutionary reform does not place the blame for our troubles on institutions but on humanity; not on how man handles his property, but on how man handles himself. This is a less popular method of reform than the first: we all prefer to blame something other than ourselves for our difficulties. The child kicks the door on which he bumped his head; the golfer breaks his club because he did not make the hole. Yet it was the golfer's fault he missed — not that of the club, nor of the God Whom he may curse, in his irritation. The world is like the golfer: man forever throws the blame for his troubles away from the one place where it belongs — himself.

Projecting the blame for our difficulties brings no solution, and it never will. For the trouble with the world lies in man. There is no point in transferring the title to property from a few capitalists to a few commissars, if you leave both groups greedy and dishonest. There is no point in tinkering with the rules of parliamentary institutions, when the trouble lies, not in the rules, but in the selfishness of the men who administer them. If we would remake the world, we must begin by remaking the individual; then the institutions will be good enough, for they will resemble the good men who made them.

And that is why institutions and plans must be

supple and elastic enough to fit the free, aspiring spirit of the men who grow and enlarge their vision as they reach toward God. No lesser goal than God Himself is great enough to demand of any man that he transform his nature; no human institution has the right to cramp his powers. Man is the highest creature on earth: he matters more than every theory, every government, every plan, for the world and all that it contains are not worth one immortal soul. Let institutions crumble, blueprints go up in smoke, and governments decay. These are mere trivia, compared to the vast question asked of all of us: "How is a man the better for it, if he gains the whole world at the cost of losing his own soul?" (cf. Mk 8:36).

37

There Is Hope

OUR WORLD IS FULL OF prophets of gloom, and I would be one of them if I did not practically believe in God. Thirty years ago the one word on everyone's lips was "progress." Now everyone speaks of defeat and the atomic bomb. This attitude of pessimism varies in direct ratio and proportion to the frequency with which one follows world news. This is not necessarily because world news is depressing, but because one seldom allows time for counterbalancing war news with other factors. As a result people lead political lives, not spiritual lives.

It would be interesting to see a commentator take the medical reports of sick patients in hospitals and broadcast them; or to read the headlines after one detail of the report was selected to the exclusion of others. We might read something like this: "Appendix lost! Life despaired!" Tremendous disproportions are created by headlines and news reports, as too often the startling is identified with the true. Parents who live in love and affection for one another, and rear their children for the triple piety of

God, neighbor, and country make no headlines. But let Glamorous Glamor separate from her husband after eighteen months of biological unity, and it becomes news. The worst is taken; the good is forgotten.

So it is with the war and the world situation. Times are bad! They have never been worse; for never before has a world civilization turned against the Divine Light. We are indeed witnessing the transfer of the Christian heritage from the West to the East. Not that the West will lose it, but that the East will begin to do with it what the West did with it in its Springtime. But despite these facts, this is not the end of civilization; nor are we to be without hope. We have simply reached a moment in history where God is permitting us to feel our inadequacy, so long as we trust only in ourselves. Very often a father will allow his son, who "thinks he knows all about it," to fumble and to err in building his playhouse, until in humility he calls upon the father to help him.

Instead of this being a time of disaster, it is rather a period of humiliation. We are being left to ourselves, to our own devices, to our own conceits. Day by day we are learning that scriptural truth: "Woe to those who go down to Egypt for help, who depend upon horses; who put their trust in chariots because of their number, and in horsemen because of their combined power, but look not to the Holy One of Israel nor seek the Lord" (Is 31:1).

A farmer went with his son into a wheat field to see if it was ready for the harvest. The son pointed to the stems that held up their heads, saying: "Those that let their heads hang cannot be good for much." The father replied: "See here, foolish child. This stalk that stands so straight is lightheaded, and almost good for nothing, while these that hang their heads so modestly are full of beautiful grain." In national life, as in nature, humility, with a head bowed before God, is the beginning of greatness.

Our greatest days are ahead, though in between intervenes the purging, where we will learn that as the rays cannot survive without the sun, so neither can we prosper without God. This hope can be translated into victory in either of two ways: by prayerfully reawakening our hearts, or by being brought within an inch of disaster, until from the depths of our insufficiency we cry out to the goodness of God. The world, and in particular our own country, is filled with thousands and thousands of good people; there is an intensification of spiritual life that is inspiring; intercession has multiplied; the young are craving for spiritual sacrifice. We are not lost! We are only losing our pride. God never puts the crown of victory on a swollen head. As the shadows of the sun are longest when its beams are lowest, so we are greatest when we make ourselves least. Pride slays thanksgiving. Our next greatest victory in making peace will be celebrated by a solemn national act of thanksgiving to God. How far away is it?